Contents

Foreword i

Testimonials ii

Education for Children iv

FAQ v

Change Log vii

How to read it? ix

What you can expect (so far...) x

Introduction to React 1
   Hi, my name is React. 2
   Requirements 4
   node and npm 5
   Installation 7
   Zero-Configuration Setup 8
   Introduction to JSX 11
   ES6 const and let 14
   ReactDOM 16
   Hot Module Replacement 17
   Complex JavaScript in JSX 19
   ES6 Arrow Functions 23
   ES6 Classes 25

Basics in React 28
   Internal Component State 29
   ES6 Object Initializer 32
   Unidirectional Data Flow 34
   Bindings 39
   Event Handler 44

CONTENTS

    Interactions with Forms and Events 49
    ES6 Destructuring 57
    Controlled Components 59
    Split Up Components 61
    Composable Components 65
    Reusable Components 67
    Component Declarations 70
    Styling Components 74

Getting Real with an API 81
    Lifecycle Methods 82
    Fetching Data 85
    ES6 Spread Operators 89
    Conditional Rendering 92
    Client- or Server-side Search 95
    Paginated Fetch 99
    Client Cache 103
    Error Handling 110

Code Organization and Testing 115
    ES6 Modules: Import and Export 116
    Code Organization with ES6 Modules 120
    Snapshot Tests with Jest 125
    Unit Tests with Enzyme 132
    Component Interface with PropTypes 134

Advanced React Components 139
    Ref a DOM Element 140
    Loading 144
    Higher Order Components 148
    Advanced Sorting 152

State Management in React and beyond 165
    Lifting State 166
    Revisited: setState() 173
    Taming the State 178

Final Steps to Production 180
    Eject 181
    Deploy your App 182

Outline 183

Foreword

The Road to learn React teaches you the fundamentals of React. You will build a real world application along the way in plain React without complicated tooling. Everything from project setup to deployment on a server will be explained. The book comes with additional referenced reading material and exercises with each chapter. After reading the book, you will be able to build your own applications in React. The material is kept up to date by me, Robin Wieruch, and the community.

In the Road to learn React, I want to offer a foundation before you start to dive into the broader React ecosystem. It has less tooling and less external state management, but a lot of information around React. It explains general concepts, patterns and best practices in a real world React application.

You will learn to build your own React application. It covers real world features like pagination, client-side caching and interactions like searching and sorting. Additionally you will transition from JavaScript ES5 to JavaScript ES6 along the way. I hope this book captures my enthusiasm for React and JavaScript and helps you to get started.

Testimonials

Muhammad Kashif[1]: "The Road to Learn React is a unique book that I recommend to any student or professional interested in learning react basics to advanced level. It is packed with insightful tips and techniques that are hard to find elsewhere, and remarkably thorough in its use of examples and references to sample problems, i have 17 years of experience in web and desktop app development, and before reading this book i was having trouble in learning react, but this book works like magic."

Andre Vargas[2]: "The Road to Learn React by Robin Wieruch is such an awesome book! Most of what I learned about React and even ES6 was through it!"

Nicholas Hunt-Walker, Instructor of Python at a Seattle Coding School[3]: "This is one of the most well-written & informative coding books I've ever worked through. A solid React & ES6 introduction."

Austin Green[4]: "Thanks, really loved the book. Perfect blend to learn React, ES6, and higher level programming concepts."

Nicole Ferguson[5]: "I'm doing Robin's Road to Learn React course this weekend & I almost feel guilty for having so much fun."

Karan[6]: "Just finished your Road to React. Best book for a beginner in the world of React and JS. Elegant exposure to ES. Kudos! :)"

Eric Priou[7]: "The Road to learn React by Robin Wieruch is a must read. Clean and concise for React and JavaScript."

A Rookie Developer: "I just finished the book as a rookie developer, thanks for working on this. It was easy to follow and I feel confident in starting a new app from scratch in the coming days. The book was much better than official React.js tutorial that I tried earlier (and couldn't complete due to lack of detail). The exercises at the end of each section were very rewarding."

Student: "The best book to start learning ReactJS. The project moves along with the concepts being learnt which helps to grasp the subject. I have found 'Code and learn' as best way to master programming and this book exactly does that."

Thomas Lockney[8]: "Pretty solid introduction to React that doesn't try to be comprehensive. I just wanted a taste to understand what it was about and this book gave me exactly that. I didn't follow all

---

[1] https://twitter.com/appsdevpk/status/848625244956901376
[2] https://twitter.com/andrevar66/status/853789166987038720
[3] https://twitter.com/nhuntwalker/status/845730837823840256
[4] https://twitter.com/AustinGreen/status/845321540627521536
[5] https://twitter.com/nicoleffe/status/833488391148822528
[6] https://twitter.com/kvss1992/status/889197346344493056
[7] https://twitter.com/erixtekila/status/840875459730657283
[8] https://www.goodreads.com/review/show/1880673388

the little footnotes to learn about the new ES6 features I've missed ("I wouldn't say I've been missing it, Bob."). But I'm sure for those of you who have fallen behind and are diligent about following those, you can probably learn a lot more than just what the book teaches."

Education for Children

The book should enable everyone to learn React. However, not everyone is privileged to use those resources, because not everyone is educated in the English language in the first place. Thus I want to use the project to support projects that teach children English in the developing world.

- 1. April to 18. April, 2017, Giving Back, By Learning React[9]

---

[9] https://www.robinwieruch.de/giving-back-by-learning-react/

FAQ

How do I get updates? You can subscribe[10] to the Newsletter or follow me on Twitter[11] for updates. Once you have a copy of the book, it will stay updated when a new edition gets released. But you have to grab the copy again when an update is announced.

Does it use the recent React version? The book always receives an update when the React version got updated. Usually books are outdated pretty soon after their release. Since this book is self-published, I can update it whenever I want.

Does it cover Redux? It doesn't. Therefore I have written a second book. The Road to learn React should give you a solid foundation before you dive into advanced topics. The implementation of the sample application in the book will show that you don't need Redux to build an application in React. After you have read the book, you should be able to implement a solid application without Redux. Then you can read my second book to learn Redux[12].

Does it use JavaScript ES6? Yes. But don't worry. You will be fine if you are familiar with JavaScript ES5. All JavaScript ES6 features, that I describe on the journey to learn React, will transition from ES5 to ES6 in the book. Every feature along the way will be explained. The book does not only teach React, but also all useful JavaScript ES6 features for React.

Will you add more chapters in the future? You can have a look at the Change Log chapter for major updates that already happened. There will be unannounced improvements in between too. In general, it depends on the community whether I continue to work on the book. If there is an acceptance for the book, I will deliver more chapters and improve the old material. I will keep the content up to date with recent best practices, concepts and patterns.

How can I get help while reading the book? The book has a Slack Group[13] for people who are reading the book. You can join the channel to get help or to help others. After all, helping others can improve your learnings too.

Is there any troubleshoot area? If you run into problems, please join the Slack Group. In addition, you could have a look into the open issues on GitHub[14] for the book. Perhaps your problem was already mentioned and you can find the solution for it. If your problem wasn't mentioned, don't hesitate to open a new issue where you can explain your problem, maybe provide a screenshot, and some more details (e.g. book page, node version). After all, I try to ship all fixes in next editions of the book.

---

[10] https://www.getrevue.co/profile/rwieruch
[11] https://twitter.com/rwieruch
[12] https://roadtoreact.com/course-details?courseId=TAMING_THE_STATE
[13] https://slack-the-road-to-learn-react.wieruch.com/
[14] https://github.com/rwieruch/the-road-to-learn-react/issues

Can I help to improve it? Yes. You can have a direct impact with your thoughts and contributions on GitHub[15]. I don't claim to be an expert nor to write in native English. I would appreciate your help very much.

Can I support the project? Yes. Feel free to reach out. I invest a lot of my time into open source tutorials and learning resources. You can have a look at my about me[16] page. I would love to have you as my Patron on Patreon[17].

Is there a call to action? Yes. I want you to take a moment to think about a person who would be a good match to learn React. The person could have shown the interest already, could be in the middle of learning React or might not yet be aware about wanting to learn React. Reach out to that person and share the book. It would mean a lot to me. The book is intended to be given to others.

---

[15] https://github.com/rwieruch/the-road-to-learn-react
[16] https://www.robinwieruch.de/about/
[17] https://www.patreon.com/rwieruch

Change Log

10. January 2017:

- v2 Pull Request[18]
- even more beginner friendly
- 37% more content
- 30% improved content
- 13 improved and new chapters
- 140 pages of learning material
- + interactive course of the book on educative.io[19]

08. March 2017:

- v3 Pull Request[20]
- 20% more content
- 25% improved content
- 9 new chapters
- 170 pages of learning material

15. April 2017:

- upgrade to React 15.5

5. July 2017:

- upgrade to node 8.1.3
- upgrade to npm 5.0.4
- upgrade to create-react-app 1.3.3

17. October 2017:

- upgrade to node 8.3.0

---

[18] https://github.com/rwieruch/the-road-to-learn-react/pull/18
[19] https://www.educative.io/collection/5740745361195008/5676830073815040
[20] https://github.com/rwieruch/the-road-to-learn-react/pull/34

- upgrade to npm 5.5.1
- upgrade to create-react-app 1.4.1
- upgrade to React 16
- v4 Pull Request[21]
- 15% more content
- 15% improved content
- 3 new chapters (Bindings, Event Handlers, Error Handling)
- 190+ pages of learning material
- +9 Source Code Projects[22]

---

[21]https://github.com/rwieruch/the-road-to-learn-react/pull/72
[22]https://roadtoreact.com/course-details?courseId=THE_ROAD_TO_LEARN_REACT

How to read it?

The book is my attempt to teach React while you will write an application. It is a practical guide to learn React and not a reference work about React. You will write a Hacker News application that interacts with a real world API. Among several interesting topics, it covers state management in React, caching and interactions (sorting and searching). On the way you will learn best practices and patterns in React.

In addition, the book gives you a transition from JavaScript ES5 to JavaScript ES6. React embraces a lot of JavaScript ES6 features and I want to show you how you can use them.

In general each chapter of the book will build up on the previous chapter. Each chapter will teach you something new. Don't rush through the book. You should internalize each step. You could apply your own implementations and read more about the topic. After each chapter I give you some reading material and exercises. If you really want to learn React, I highly recommend to read the extra material and do some hands on exercises. After you have read a chapter, make yourself comfortable with the learnings before you continue.

In the end you will have a complete React application in production. I am very keen to see your results, so please text me when you have finished the book. The final chapter of the book will give you a handful of options to continue your React journey. In general you will find a lot of React related topics on my personal website[23].

Since you are reading the book, I guess you are new to React. That's perfect. In the end I hope to get your feedback to improve the material to enable everyone to learn React. You can have a direct impact on GitHub[24] or text me on Twitter[25].

---

[23] https://www.robinwieruch.de/
[24] https://github.com/rwieruch/the-road-to-learn-react
[25] https://twitter.com/rwieruch

What you can expect (so far...)

- Hacker News App in React[26]
- no complicated configurations
- create-react-app to bootstrap your application
- efficient lightweight code
- only React setState as state management (so far...)
- transition from JavaScript ES5 to ES6 along the way
- the React API with setState and lifecycle methods
- interaction with a real world API (Hacker News)
- advanced user interactions
  - client-sided sorting
  - client-sided filtering
  - server-sided searching
- implementation of client-side caching
- higher order functions and higher order components
- snapshot test components with Jest
- unit test components with Enzyme
- neat libraries along the way
- exercises and more readings along the way
- internalize and reinforce your learnings
- deploy your application to production

---

[26]https://intense-refuge-78753.herokuapp.com/

Introduction to React

The chapter gives you an introduction to React. You may ask yourself: Why should I learn React in the first place? The chapter might give you the answer to that question. Afterward, you will dive into the ecosystem by bootstrapping your first React application from scratch with zero-configuration. Along the way, you will get an introduction to JSX and ReactDOM. So be prepared for your first React components.

Hi, my name is React.

Why should you bother to learn React? In recent years single page applications (SPA[27]) have become popular. Frameworks like Angular, Ember and Backbone helped JavaScript developers to build modern web applications beyond the usage of vanilla JavaScript and jQuery. The list of these popular solutions is not exhaustive. There exists a wide range of SPA frameworks. When you consider the release dates, most of them are among the first generation of SPAs: Angular 2010, Backbone 2010 and Ember 2011.

The initial React release was 2013 by Facebook. React is not an SPA framework but a view library. It is the V in the MVC[28] (model view controller). It only enables you to render components as viewable elements in a browser. Yet the whole ecosystem around React makes it possible to build single page applications.

But why should you consider using React over the first generation of SPA frameworks? While the first generation of frameworks tried to solve a lot of things at once, React only helps you to build your view layer. It's a library and not a framework. The idea behind it: Your view is a hierarchy of composable components.

In React you can keep the focus on your view layer before you introduce more aspects to your application. Every other aspect is another building block for your SPA. These building blocks are essential to build a mature application. They come with two advantages.

First, you can learn the building blocks step by step. You don't have to worry about understanding them altogether. It is different from a framework that gives you every building block from the start. This book focuses on React as the first building block. More building blocks follow eventually.

Second, all building blocks are interchangeable. It makes the ecosystem around React such an innovative place. Multiple solutions are competing with each other. You can pick the most appealing solution for you and your use case.

The first generation of SPA frameworks arrived at an enterprise level. They are more rigid. React stays innovative and gets adopted by multiple tech thought leader companies like Airbnb, Netflix and of course Facebook[29]. All of them invest in the future of React and are content with React and the ecosystem itself.

React is probably one of the best choices for building modern web applications nowadays. It only delivers the view layer, but the React ecosystem is a whole flexible and interchangeable framework[30]. React has a slim API, an amazing ecosystem and a great community. You can read about my experiences why I moved from Angular to React[31]. I highly recommend to have an understanding why you would choose React over another framework or library. After all, everyone is keen to experience where React will lead us in the next years.

---

[27] https://en.wikipedia.org/wiki/Single-page_application
[28] https://de.wikipedia.org/wiki/Model_View_Controller
[29] https://github.com/facebook/react/wiki/Sites-Using-React
[30] https://www.robinwieruch.de/essential-react-libraries-framework/
[31] https://www.robinwieruch.de/reasons-why-i-moved-from-angular-to-react/

Exercises

- read about why I moved from Angular to React[32]
- read about React's flexible ecosystem[33]

---

[32] https://www.robinwieruch.de/reasons-why-i-moved-from-angular-to-react/
[33] https://www.robinwieruch.de/essential-react-libraries-framework/

Requirements

If you are coming from a different SPA framework or library, you should already be familiar with the basics of web development. If you have just started in web development, you should feel comfortable with HTML, CSS and JavaScript ES5 to learn React. The book will smoothly transition to JavaScript ES6 and beyond. I encourage you to join the official Slack Group[34] for the book to get help or to help others.

Editor and Terminal

What about the development environment? You will need a running editor or IDE and terminal (command line tool). You can follow my setup guide[35]. It is adjusted for MacOS users, but you can substitute most of the tools for other operating system. There is a ton of articles out there that will show you how to setup a web development environment in a more elaborated way for your OS.

Optionally, you can use git and GitHub on your own, while conducting the exercises in the book, to keep your projects and the progress in repositories on GitHub. There exists a little guide[36] on how to use these tools. But once again, it is not mandatory for the book and can be overwhelming when learning everything from scratch. So you can skip it if you are a newcomer in web development to focus on the essential parts taught in this book.

Node and NPM

Last but not least, you will need an installation of node and npm[37]. Both are used to manage libraries you will need along the way. In this book, you will install external node packages via npm (node package manager). These node packages can be libraries or whole frameworks.

You can verify your versions of node and npm on the command line. If you don't get any output in the terminal, you need to install node and npm first. These are only my versions during the time writing this book:

Command Line

```
node --version
*v8.3.0
npm --version
*v5.5.1
```

---

[34] https://slack-the-road-to-learn-react.wieruch.com/
[35] https://www.robinwieruch.de/developer-setup/
[36] https://www.robinwieruch.de/git-essential-commands/
[37] https://nodejs.org/en/

Introduction to React

node and npm

This chapter gives you a little crash course in node and npm. It is not exhaustive, but you will get all the necessary tools. If you are familiar with both of them, you can skip the chapter.

The **node package manager** (npm) allows you to install external **node packages** from the command line. These packages can be a set of utility functions, libraries or whole frameworks. They are the dependencies of your application. You can either install these packages to your global node package folder or to your local project folder.

Global node packages are accessible from everywhere in the terminal and you have to install them only once to your global directory. You can install a global package by typing in your terminal:

Command Line

```
npm install -g <package>
```

The -g flag tells npm to install the package globally. Local packages are used in your application. For instance, React as a library will be a local package which can be required in your application for usage. You can install it via the terminal by typing:

Command Line

```
npm install <package>
```

In the case of React it would be:

Command Line

```
npm install react
```

The installed package will automatically appear in a folder called *node_modules/* and will be listed in the *package.json* file next to your other dependencies.

But how to initialize the *node_modules/* folder and the *package.json* file for your project in the first place? There is a npm command to initialize a npm project and thus a *package.json* file. Only when you have that file, you can install new local packages via npm.

Command Line

```
npm init -y
```

Introduction to React

The -y flag is a shortcut to initialize all the defaults in your *package.json*. If you don't use the flag, you have to decide how to configure the file. After initializing your npm project you are good to install new packages via `npm install <package>`.

One more word about the *package.json*. The file enables you to share your project with other developers without sharing all the node packages. The file has all the references of node packages used in your project. These packages are called dependencies. Everyone can copy your project without the dependencies. The dependencies are references in the *package.json*. Someone who copies your project can simply install all packages by using `npm install` on the command line. The npm install script takes all the dependencies listed in the *package.json* file and installs them in the *node_modules/* folder.

I want to cover one more npm command:

Command Line

```
npm install --save-dev <package>
```

The `--save-dev` flag indicates that the node package is only used in the development environment. It will not be used in production when you deploy your application on a server. What kind of node package could that be? Imagine you want to test your application with the help of a node package. You need to install that package via npm, but want to exclude it from your production environment. Testing should only happen during the development process but not when your application is already running in production. There you don't want to test your application anymore. It should be tested already and work out of the box for your users. That's only one use case where you would want to use the `--save-dev` flag.

You will encounter more npm commands on your way. But these will be sufficient for now.

Exercises:

- setup a throw away npm project
    - create a new folder with `mkdir <folder_name>`
    - navigate into the folder with `cd <folder_name>`
    - execute `npm init -y` or `npm init`
    - install a local package like React with `npm install react`
    - have a look into the *package.json* file and the *node_modules/* folder
    - find out on your own how to uninstall the *react* node package again
- read more about npm[38]

---

[38] https://docs.npmjs.com/

Installation

There are multiple approaches to get started with a React application.

The first one is to use a CDN. That may sound more complicated than it is. A CDN is a content delivery network[39]. Several companies have CDNs that host files publicly for people to consume them. These files can be libraries like React, because after all the bundled React library is only a *react.js* JavaScript file. It can be hosted somewhere and you can require it in your application.

How to use a CDN to get started in React? You can inline the `<script>` tag in your HTML that points to a CDN url. To get started in React you need two files (libraries): *react* and *react-dom*.

Code Playground
```
<script crossorigin src="https://unpkg.com/react@16/umd/react.development.js"></\
script>
<script crossorigin src="https://unpkg.com/react-dom@16/umd/react-dom.developmen\
t.js"></script>
```

But why should you use a CDN when you have npm to install node packages such as React?

When your application has a *package.json* file, you can install *react* and *react-dom* from the command line. The requirement is that the folder is initialized as npm project by using `npm init -y` with a *package.json* file. You can install multiple node packages in one line with npm.

Command Line
```
npm install react react-dom
```

That approach is often used to add React to an existing application that is managed with npm.

Unfortunately that's not everything. You would have to deal with Babel[40] to make your application aware of JSX (the React syntax) and JavaScript ES6. Babel transpiles your code so that browsers can interpret JavaScript ES6 and JSX. Not all browsers are capable of interpreting the syntax. The setup includes a lot of configuration and tooling. It can be overwhelming for React newcomers to bother with all the configuration.

Because of this reason, Facebook introduced *create-react-app* as a zero-configuration React solution. The next chapter will show you how to setup your application by using this bootstrapping tool.

Exercises:

- read more about React installations[41]

---

[39] https://en.wikipedia.org/wiki/Content_delivery_network
[40] http://babeljs.io/
[41] https://facebook.github.io/react/docs/installation.html

Zero-Configuration Setup

In the Road to learn React, you will use create-react-app[42] to bootstrap your application. It's an opinionated yet zero-configuration starter kit for React introduced by Facebook in 2016. People would recommend it to beginners by 96%[43]. In *create-react-app* the tooling and configuration evolve in the background while the focus is on the application implementation.

To get started, you will have to install the package to your global node packages. After that, you always have it available on the command line to bootstrap new React applications.

Command Line

```
npm install -g create-react-app
```

You can check the version of *create-react-app* to verify a successful installation on your command line:

Command Line

```
create-react-app --version
*v1.4.1
```

Now you can bootstrap your first React application. We call it *hackernews*, but you can choose a different name. The bootstrapping takes a couple of seconds. Afterward, simply navigate into the folder:

Command Line

```
create-react-app hackernews
cd hackernews
```

Now you can open the application in your editor. The following folder structure, or a variation of it depending on the *create-react-app* version, should be presented to you:

---

[42]https://github.com/facebookincubator/create-react-app
[43]https://twitter.com/dan_abramov/status/806985854099062785

Introduction to React 9

Folder Structure

```
hackernews/
  README.md
  node_modules/
  package.json
  .gitignore
  public/
    favicon.ico
    index.html
  src/
    App.css
    App.js
    App.test.js
    index.css
    index.js
    logo.svg
```

A short break down of the folder and files. It is fine if you don't understand all of them in the beginning.

- **README.md:** The .md extension indicates that the file is a markdown file. Markdown is used as a lightweight markup language with plain text formatting syntax. Many source code projects come with a *README.md* file to give you initial instructions about the project. When pushing your project to a platform such as GitHub eventually, the *README.md* file will show its content prominently when you access the repository. Because you have used *create-react-app*, your *README.md* should be the same as shown in the official create-react-app GitHub repository[44].
- **node_modules/:** The folder has all the node packages that were and are installed via npm. Since you have used *create-react-app*, there should be already a couple of node modules installed for you. Usually you will never touch this folder, but only install and uninstall node packages with npm from the command line.
- **package.json:** The file shows you a list of node package dependencies and other project configuration.
- **.gitignore:** The file indicates all files and folders that shouldn't be added to your remote git repository when using git. They should only live in your local project. The *node_modules/* folder is such a use case. It is sufficient to share the *package.json* file with your peers to enable them to install all dependencies on their own without sharing the whole dependency folder.

---

[44]https://github.com/facebookincubator/create-react-app

- **public/**: The folder holds all your files when building your project for production. Eventually all your written code in the *src/* folder will be bundled into a couple of files when building your project and placed in the public folder.

After all, you don't need to touch the mentioned files and folders. In the beginning everything you need is located in the *src/* folder. The main focus lies on the *src/App.js* file to implement React components. It will be used to implement your application, but later you might want to split up your components into multiple files whereas each file maintains one or a few components on its own.

Additionally, you will find a *src/App.test.js* file for your tests and a *src/index.js* as entry point to the React world. You will get to know both files in a later chapter. In addition, there is a *src/index.css* and a *src/App.css* file to style your general application and your components. They all come with default style when you open them.

The *create-react-app* application is a npm project. You can use npm to install and uninstall node packages to your project. Additionally it comes with the following npm scripts for your command line:

Command Line

```
// Runs the application in http://localhost:3000
npm start

// Runs the tests
npm test

// Builds the application for production
npm run build
```

The scripts are defined in your *package.json*. Your boilerplate React application is bootstrapped now. The exciting part comes in the exercises to finally run your bootstrapped application in the browser.

Exercises:

- `npm start` your application and visit the application in your browser
- run the interactive `npm test` script
- check the content of your *public/* folder, run the `npm run build` script and verify that files were added to the folder (you can remove these files again, but they don't do any harm)
- make yourself familiar with the folder structure
- make yourself familiar with the content of the files
- read more about the npm scripts and create-react-app[45]

---

[45] https://github.com/facebookincubator/create-react-app

Introduction to JSX

Now you will get to know JSX. It is the syntax in React. As mentioned before, *create-react-app* has already bootstrapped a boilerplate application for you. All files come with default implementations. Let's dive into the source code. The only file you will touch in the beginning will be the *src/App.js* file.

src/App.js

```
import React, { Component } from 'react';
import logo from './logo.svg';
import './App.css';

class App extends Component {
  render() {
    return (
      <div className="App">
        <header className="App-header">
          <img src={logo} className="App-logo" alt="logo" />
          <h1 className="App-title">Welcome to React</h1>
        </header>
        <p className="App-intro">
          To get started, edit <code>src/App.js</code> and save to reload.
        </p>
      </div>
    );
  }
}

export default App;
```

Don't let yourself get confused by the import/export statements and class declaration. These features are already JavaScript ES6. We will revisit those in a later chapter.

In the file you have an **React ES6 class component** with the name App. It is a component declaration. Basically after you have declared a component, you can use it as element everywhere in your application. It will produce an **instance** of your **component** or in other words: the component gets instantiated.

The **element** it returns is specified in the render() method. Elements are what components are made of. It is useful to understand the differences between component, instance and element.

Pretty soon, you will see where the App component is instantiated. Otherwise you wouldn't see the rendered output in the browser, would you? The App component is only the declaration, but not the usage. You would instantiate the component somewhere in your JSX with <App />.

The content in the render block looks pretty similar to HTML, but it's JSX. JSX allows you to mix HTML and JavaScript. It's powerful yet confusing when you are used to separate your HTML and JavaScript. That's why a good starting point is to use basic HTML in your JSX. In the beginning, remove all the distracting content in the file.

src/App.js

```
import React, { Component } from 'react';
import './App.css';

class App extends Component {
  render() {
    return (
      <div className="App">
        <h2>Welcome to the Road to learn React</h2>
      </div>
    );
  }
}

export default App;
```

Now, you only return HTML in your `render()` method without JavaScript. Let's define the "Welcome to the Road to learn React" as a variable. A variable can be used in your JSX by using curly braces.

src/App.js

```
import React, { Component } from 'react';
import './App.css';

class App extends Component {
  render() {
    var helloWorld = 'Welcome to the Road to learn React';
    return (
      <div className="App">
        <h2>{helloWorld}</h2>
      </div>
    );
  }
}

export default App;
```

Introduction to React

It should work when you start your application on the command line with npm start again.

Additionally you might have noticed the className attribute. It reflects the standard class attribute in HTML. Because of technical reasons, JSX had to replace a handful of internal HTML attributes. You can find all of the supported HTML attributes in the React documentation[46]. They all follow the camelCase convention. On your way to learn React, you will come across some more JSX specific attributes.

Exercises:

- define more variables and render them in your JSX
    - use a complex object to represent an user with a first name and last name
    - render the user properties in your JSX
- read more about JSX[47]
- read more about React components, elements and instances[48]

---

[46] https://facebook.github.io/react/docs/dom-elements.html
[47] https://facebook.github.io/react/docs/introducing-jsx.html
[48] https://facebook.github.io/react/blog/2015/12/18/react-components-elements-and-instances.html

ES6 const and let

I guess you noticed that we declared the variable `helloWorld` with a `var` statement. JavaScript ES6 comes with two more options to declare your variables: `const` and `let`. In JavaScript ES6, you will rarely find `var` anymore.

A variable declared with `const` cannot be re-assigned or re-declared. It cannot get mutated (changed, modified). You embrace immutable data structures by using it. Once the data structure is defined, you cannot change it.

Code Playground
```
// not allowed
const helloWorld = 'Welcome to the Road to learn React';
helloWorld = 'Bye Bye React';
```

A variable declared with `let` can get mutated.

Code Playground
```
// allowed
let helloWorld = 'Welcome to the Road to learn React';
helloWorld = 'Bye Bye React';
```

You would use it when you would need to re-assign a variable.

However, you have to be careful with `const`. A variable declared with `const` cannot get modified. But when the variable is an array or object, the value it holds can get updated. The value it holds is not immutable.

Code Playground
```
// allowed
const helloWorld = {
  text: 'Welcome to the Road to learn React'
};
helloWorld.text = 'Bye Bye React';
```

But when to use each declaration? There are different opinions about the usage. I suggest using `const` whenever you can. It indicates that you want to keep your data structure immutable even though values in objects and arrays can get modified. If you want to modify your variable, you can use `let`.

Immutability is embraced in React and its ecosystem. That's why `const` should be your default choice when you define a variable. Still, in complex objects the values within can get modified. Be careful about this behavior.

In your application, you should use `const` over `var`.

Introduction to React

src/App.js

```
import React, { Component } from 'react';
import './App.css';

class App extends Component {
  render() {
    const helloWorld = 'Welcome to the Road to learn React';
    return (
      <div className="App">
        <h2>{helloWorld}</h2>
      </div>
    );
  }
}

export default App;
```

Exercises:

- read more about ES6 const[49]
- read more about ES6 let[50]
- research more about immutable data structures
    - why do they make sense in programming in general
    - why are they used in React and its ecosystem

---

[49]https://developer.mozilla.org/en-US/docs/Web/JavaScript/Reference/Statements/const
[50]https://developer.mozilla.org/en-US/docs/Web/JavaScript/Reference/Statements/let

ReactDOM

Before you continue with the App component, you might want to see where it is used. It is located in your entry point to the React world: the *src/index.js* file.

src/index.js

```
import React from 'react';
import ReactDOM from 'react-dom';
import App from './App';
import './index.css';

ReactDOM.render(
  <App />,
  document.getElementById('root')
);
```

Basically `ReactDOM.render()` uses a DOM node in your HTML to replace it with your JSX. That's how you can easily integrate React in every foreign application. It is not forbidden to use `ReactDOM.render()` multiple times across your application. You can use it at multiple places to bootstrap simple JSX syntax, a React component, multiple React components or a whole application. But in plain React application you will only use it once to bootstrap your whole component tree.

`ReactDOM.render()` expects two arguments. The first argument is JSX that gets rendered. The second argument specifies the place where the React application hooks into your HTML. It expects an element with an `id='root'`. You can open your *public/index.html* file to find the id attribute.

In the implementation `ReactDOM.render()` already takes your App component. However, it would be fine to pass simpler JSX as long as it is JSX. It doesn't have to be an instantiation of a component.

Code Playground

```
ReactDOM.render(
  <h1>Hello React World</h1>,
  document.getElementById('root')
);
```

Exercises:

- open the *public/index.html* to see where the React applications hooks into your HTML
- read more about rendering elements in React[51]

---

[51] https://facebook.github.io/react/docs/rendering-elements.html

Hot Module Replacement

There is one thing that you can do in the *src/index.js* file to improve your development experience as a developer. But it is optional and shouldn't overwhelm you in the beginning when learning React.

In *create-react-app* it is already an advantage that the browser automatically refreshes the page when you change your source code. Try it by changing the `helloWorld` variable in your *src/App.js* file. The browser should refresh the page. But there is a better way of doing it.

Hot Module Replacement (HMR) is a tool to reload your application in the browser. The browser doesn't perform a page refresh. You can easily activate it in *create-react-app*. In your *src/index.js*, your entry point to React, you have to add one little configuration.

src/index.js

```
import React from 'react';
import ReactDOM from 'react-dom';
import App from './App';
import './index.css';

ReactDOM.render(
  <App />,
  document.getElementById('root')
);

if (module.hot) {
  module.hot.accept();
}
```

That's it. Try again to change the `helloWorld` variable in your *src/App.js* file. The browser shouldn't perform a page refresh, but the application reloads and shows the correct output. HMR comes with multiple advantages:

Imagine you are debugging your code with `console.log()` statements. These statements will stay in your developer console, even though you change your code, because the browser doesn't refresh the page anymore. That can be convenient for debugging purposes.

In a growing application a page refresh delays your productivity. You have to wait until the page loads. A page reload can take several seconds in a large application. HMR takes away this disadvantage.

The biggest benefit is that you can keep the application state with HMR. Imagine you have a dialog in your application with multiple steps and you are at step 3. Basically it is a wizard. Without HMR you would change the source code and your browser refreshes the page. You would have to open the dialog again and would have to navigate from step 1 to step 3. With HMR your dialog stays open at step 3. It keeps the application state even though the source code changes. The application itself reloads, but not the page.

Exercises:

- change your *src/App.js* source code a few times to see HMR in action
- watch the first 10 minutes of Live React: Hot Reloading with Time Travel[52] by Dan Abramov

---

[52] https://www.youtube.com/watch?v=xsSnOQynTHs

Complex JavaScript in JSX

Let's get back to your App component. So far you rendered some primitive variables in your JSX. Now you will start to render a list of items. The list will be sample data in the beginning, but later you will fetch the data from an external API[53]. That will be far more exciting.

First you have to define the list of items.

src/App.js
```
import React, { Component } from 'react';
import './App.css';

const list = [
  {
    title: 'React',
    url: 'https://facebook.github.io/react/',
    author: 'Jordan Walke',
    num_comments: 3,
    points: 4,
    objectID: 0,
  },
  {
    title: 'Redux',
    url: 'https://github.com/reactjs/redux',
    author: 'Dan Abramov, Andrew Clark',
    num_comments: 2,
    points: 5,
    objectID: 1,
  },
];

class App extends Component {
  ...
}
```

The sample data will reflect the data we will fetch later on from the API. An item in the list has a title, an url and an author. Additionally it comes with an identifier, points (which indicate how popular an article is) and a count of comments.

Now you can use the built-in JavaScript map functionality in your JSX. It enables you to iterate over your list of items to display them. Again you will use curly braces to encapsulate the JavaScript expression in your JSX.

[53] https://www.robinwieruch.de/what-is-an-api-javascript/

Introduction to React

src/App.js

```
class App extends Component {
  render() {
    return (
      <div className="App">
        {list.map(function(item) {
          return <div>{item.title}</div>;
        })}
      </div>
    );
  }
}

export default App;
```

Using JavaScript in HTML is pretty powerful in JSX. Usually you might have used map to convert one list of items to another list of items. This time you use map to convert a list of items to HTML elements.

So far, only the title will be displayed for each item. Let's display some more of the item properties.

src/App.js

```
class App extends Component {
  render() {
    return (
      <div className="App">
        {list.map(function(item) {
          return (
            <div>
              <span>
                <a href={item.url}>{item.title}</a>
              </span>
              <span>{item.author}</span>
              <span>{item.num_comments}</span>
              <span>{item.points}</span>
            </div>
          );
        })}
      </div>
    );
  }
}
```

}

```
export default App;
```

You can see how the map function is simply inlined in your JSX. Each item property is displayed in a `<span>` tag. Moreover the url property of the item is used in the `href` attribute of the anchor tag.

React will do all the work for you and display each item. But you should add one helper for React to embrace its full potential and improve its performance. You have to assign a key attribute to each list element. That way React is able to identify added, changed and removed items when the list changes. The sample list items come with an identifier already.

src/App.js

```
{list.map(function(item) {
  return (
    <div key={item.objectID}>
      <span>
        <a href={item.url}>{item.title}</a>
      </span>
      <span>{item.author}</span>
      <span>{item.num_comments}</span>
      <span>{item.points}</span>
    </div>
  );
})}
```

You should make sure that the key attribute is a stable identifier. Don't make the mistake of using index of the item in the array. The array index isn't stable at all. For instance, when the list changes its order, React will have a hard time identifying the items properly.

src/App.js

```
// don't do this
{list.map(function(item, key) {
  return (
    <div key={key}>
      ...
    </div>
  );
})}
```

You are displaying both list items now. You can start your app, open your browser and see both items of the list displayed.

Exercises:

- read more about React lists and keys[54]
- recap the standard built-in array functionalities in JavaScript[55]
- use more JavaScript expressions on your own in JSX

---

[54]https://facebook.github.io/react/docs/lists-and-keys.html
[55]https://developer.mozilla.org/en-US/docs/Web/JavaScript/Reference/Global_Objects/Array/map

ES6 Arrow Functions

JavaScript ES6 introduced arrow functions. An arrow function expression is shorter than a function expression.

Code Playground

```
// function expression
function () { ... }

// arrow function expression
() => { ... }
```

But you have to be aware of its functionalities. One of them is a different behavior with the `this` object. A function expression always defines its own `this` object. Arrow function expressions have the `this` object of the enclosing context. Don't get confused when using `this` in an arrow function.

There is another valuable fact about arrow functions regarding the parenthesis. You can remove the parenthesis when the function gets only one argument, but have to keep them when it gets multiple arguments.

Code Playground

```
// allowed
item => { ... }

// allowed
(item) => { ... }

// not allowed
item, key => { ... }

// allowed
(item, key) => { ... }
```

However, let's have a look at the `map` function. You can write it more concisely with an ES6 arrow function.

src/App.js

```
list.map(item => {
  return (
    <div key={item.objectID}>
      <span>
        <a href={item.url}>{item.title}</a>
      </span>
      <span>{item.author}</span>
      <span>{item.num_comments}</span>
      <span>{item.points}</span>
    </div>
  );
})}
```

Additionally, you can remove the *block body*, meaning the curly braces, of the ES6 arrow function. In a *concise body* an implicit return is attached. Thus you can remove the return statement. That will happen more often in the book, so be sure to understand the difference between a block body and a concise body when using arrow functions.

src/App.js

```
{list.map(item =>
  <div key={item.objectID}>
    <span>
      <a href={item.url}>{item.title}</a>
    </span>
    <span>{item.author}</span>
    <span>{item.num_comments}</span>
    <span>{item.points}</span>
  </div>
)}
```

Your JSX looks more concise and readable now. It omits the function statement, the curly braces and the return statement. Instead a developer can focus on the implementation details.

Exercises:

- read more about ES6 arrow functions[56]

---

[56]https://developer.mozilla.org/en/docs/Web/JavaScript/Reference/Functions/Arrow_functions

ES6 Classes

JavaScript ES6 introduced classes. A class is commonly used in object-oriented programming languages. JavaScript was and is very flexible in its programming paradigms. You can do functional programming and object-oriented programming side by side for their particular use cases.

Even though React embraces functional programming, for instance with immutable data structures, classes are used to declare components. They are called ES6 class components. React mixes the good parts of both programming paradigms.

Let's consider the following Developer class to examine a JavaScript ES6 class without thinking about a component.

Code Playground

```
class Developer {
  constructor(firstname, lastname) {
    this.firstname = firstname;
    this.lastname = lastname;
  }

  getName() {
    return this.firstname + ' ' + this.lastname;
  }
}
```

A class has a constructor to make it instantiable. The constructor can take arguments to assign it to the class instance. Additionally a class can define functions. Because the function is associated with a class, it is called a method. Often it is referenced as a class method.

The Developer class is only the class declaration. You can create multiple instances of the class by invoking it. It is similar to the ES6 class component, that has a declaration, but you have to use it somewhere else to instantiate it.

Let's see how you can instantiate the class and how you can use its methods.

Code Playground

```
const robin = new Developer('Robin', 'Wieruch');
console.log(robin.getName());
// output: Robin Wieruch
```

React uses JavaScript ES6 classes for ES6 class components. You already used one ES6 class component.

src/App.js

```
import React, { Component } from 'react';

...

class App extends Component {
  render() {
    ...
  }
}
```

The App class extends from Component. Basically you declare the App component, but it extends from another component. What does extend mean? In object-oriented programming you have the principle of inheritance. It is used to pass over functionalities from one class to another class.

The App class extends functionality from the Component class. To be more specific, it inherits functionalities from the Component class. The Component class is used to extend a basic ES6 class to a ES6 component class. It has all the functionalities that a component in React needs to have. The render method is one of these functionalities that you have already used. You will learn about other component class methods later on.

The Component class encapsulates all the implementation details of a React component. It enables developers to use classes as components in React.

The methods a React Component exposes is the public interface. One of these methods has to be overridden, the others don't need to be overridden. You will learn about the latter ones when the book arrives at lifecycle methods in a later chapter. The render() method has to be overridden, because it defines the output of a React Component. It has to be defined.

Now you know the basics around JavaScript ES6 classes and how they are used in React to extend them to components. You will learn more about the Component methods when the book describes React lifecycle methods.

Exercises:

- read more about ES6 classes[57]

---

[57] https://developer.mozilla.org/en/docs/Web/JavaScript/Reference/Classes

Introduction to React

You have learned to bootstrap your own React application! Let's recap the last chapters:

- React
    - create-react-app bootstraps a React application
    - JSX mixes up HTML and JavaScript to define the output of React components in their render methods
    - components, instances and elements are different things in React
    - `ReactDOM.render()` is an entry point for a React application to hook React into the DOM
    - built-in JavaScript functionalities can be used in JSX
        * map can be used to render a list of items as HTML elements
- ES6
    - variable declarations with `const` and `let` can be used for specific use cases
        * use const over let in React applications
    - arrow functions can be used to keep your functions concise
    - classes are used to define components in React by extending them

It makes sense to take a break at this point. Internalize the learnings and apply them on your own. You can experiment with the source code you have written so far.

You can find the source code in the official repository[58].

---
[58] https://github.com/rwieruch/hackernews-client/tree/4.1

Basics in React

The chapter will guide you through the basics of React. It covers state and interactions in components, because static components are a bit dull, aren't they? Additionally, you will learn about the different ways to declare a component and how to keep components composable and reusable. Be prepared to breathe life into your components.

Internal Component State

Internal component state, also known as local state, allows you to save, modify and delete properties that are stored in your component. The ES6 class component can use a constructor to initialize internal component state later on. The constructor is called only once when the component initializes.

Let's introduce a class constructor.

src/App.js

```
class App extends Component {

  constructor(props) {
    super(props);
  }

  ...

}
```

When having a constructor in your ES6 class component, it is mandatory to call `super()`; because the App component is a subclass of `Component`. Hence the `extends Component` in your App component declaration. You will learn more about ES6 class components later on.

You can call `super(props);` as well. It sets `this.props` in your constructor in case you want to access them in the constructor. Otherwise, when accessing `this.props` in your constructor, they would be `undefined`. You will learn more about the props of a React component later on.

Now, in your case, the initial state in your component should be the sample list of items.

src/App.js

```
const list = [
  {
    title: 'React',
    url: 'https://facebook.github.io/react/',
    author: 'Jordan Walke',
    num_comments: 3,
    points: 4,
    objectID: 0,
  },
  ...
];
```

Basics in React

```
class App extends Component {

  constructor(props) {
    super(props);

    this.state = {
      list: list,
    };
  }

  ...

}
```

The state is bound to the class by using the `this` object. Thus you can access the local state in your whole component. For instance, it can be used in the `render()` method. Previously you have mapped a static list of items in your `render()` method that was defined outside of your component. Now you are about to use the list from your local state in your component.

src/App.js

```
class App extends Component {

  ...

  render() {
    return (
      <div className="App">
        {this.state.list.map(item =>
          <div key={item.objectID}>
            <span>
              <a href={item.url}>{item.title}</a>
            </span>
            <span>{item.author}</span>
            <span>{item.num_comments}</span>
            <span>{item.points}</span>
          </div>
        )}
      </div>
    );
  }
}
```

Basics in React

The list is part of the component now. It resides in the internal component state. You could add items, change items or remove items in and from your list. Every time you change your component state, the `render()` method of your component will run again. That's how you can simply change your internal component state and be sure that the component re-renders and displays the correct data that comes from the local state.

But be careful. Don't mutate the state directly. You have to use a method called `setState()` to modify your state. You will get to know it in a following chapter.

Exercises:

- experiment with the local state
    - define more initial state in the constructor
    - use and access the state in your `render()` method
- read more about the ES6 class constructor[59]

---

[59] https://developer.mozilla.org/en/docs/Web/JavaScript/Reference/Classes#Constructor

ES6 Object Initializer

In JavaScript ES6, you can use a shorthand property syntax to initialize your objects more concisely. Imagine the following object initialization:

Code Playground

```
const name = 'Robin';

const user = {
  name: name,
};
```

When the property name in your object is the same as your variable name, you can do the following:

Code Playground

```
const name = 'Robin';

const user = {
  name,
};
```

In your application, you can do the same. The list variable name and the state property name share the same name.

Code Playground

```
// ES5
this.state = {
  list: list,
};

// ES6
this.state = {
  list,
};
```

Another neat helper are shorthand method names. In JavaScript ES6, you can initialize methods in an object more concisely.

Basics in React

Code Playground

```
// ES5
var userService = {
  getUserName: function (user) {
    return user.firstname + ' ' + user.lastname;
  },
};

// ES6
const userService = {
  getUserName(user) {
    return user.firstname + ' ' + user.lastname;
  },
};
```

Last but not least, you are allowed to use computed property names in JavaScript ES6.

Code Playground

```
// ES5
var user = {
  name: 'Robin',
};

// ES6
const key = 'name';
const user = {
  [key]: 'Robin',
};
```

Perhaps computed property names make no sense for you yet. Why should you need them? In a later chapter, you will come to a point where you can use them to allocate values by key in a dynamic way in an object. It's neat to generate lookup tables in JavaScript.

Exercises:

- experiment with ES6 object initializer
- read more about ES6 object initializer[60]

---

[60] https://developer.mozilla.org/en/docs/Web/JavaScript/Reference/Operators/Object_initializer

Unidirectional Data Flow

Now you have some internal state in your App component. However, you have not manipulated the local state yet. The state is static and thus is the component. A good way to experience state manipulation is to have some component interaction.

Let's add a button for each item in the displayed list. The button says "Dismiss" and is going to remove the item from the list. It could be useful eventually when you only want to keep a list of unread items and dismiss the items that you are not interested in.

src/App.js
```
class App extends Component {

  ...

  render() {
    return (
      <div className="App">
        {this.state.list.map(item =>
          <div key={item.objectID}>
            <span>
              <a href={item.url}>{item.title}</a>
            </span>
            <span>{item.author}</span>
            <span>{item.num_comments}</span>
            <span>{item.points}</span>
            <span>
              <button
                onClick={() => this.onDismiss(item.objectID)}
                type="button"
              >
                Dismiss
              </button>
            </span>
          </div>
        )}
      </div>
    );
  }
}
```

The onDismiss() class method is not defined yet. We will do it in a moment, but for now the focus should be on the onClick handler of the button element. As you can see, the onDismiss() method

Basics in React

in the `onClick` handler is enclosed by another function. It is an arrow function. That way, you can sneak in the `objectID` property of the `item` object to identify the item that will be dismissed. An alternative way would be to define the function outside of the `onClick` handler and only pass the defined function to the handler. A later chapter will explain the topic of handlers in elements in more detail.

Did you notice the multilines for the button element? Note that elements with multiple attributes get messy as one line at some point. That's why the button element is used with multilines and indentations to keep it readable. But it is not mandatory. It is only a code style recommendation that I highly recommend.

Now you have to implement the `onDismiss()` functionality. It takes an id to identify the item to dismiss. The function is bound to the class and thus becomes a class method. That's why you access it with `this.onDismiss()` and not `onDismiss()`. The `this` object is your class instance. In order to define the `onDismiss()` as class method, you have to bind it in the constructor. Bindings will be explained in another chapter later on.

src/App.js

```
class App extends Component {

  constructor(props) {
    super(props);

    this.state = {
      list,
    };

    this.onDismiss = this.onDismiss.bind(this);
  }

  render() {
    ...
  }
}
```

In the next step, you have to define its functionality, the business logic, in your class. Class methods can be defined the following way.

src/App.js

```
class App extends Component {

  constructor(props) {
    super(props);

    this.state = {
      list,
    };

    this.onDismiss = this.onDismiss.bind(this);
  }

  onDismiss(id) {
    ...
  }

  render() {
    ...
  }
}
```

Now you are able to define what happens inside of the class method. Basically you want to remove the item identified by the id from the list and store an updated list to your local state. Afterward, the updated list will be used in the re-running `render()` method to display it. The removed item shouldn't appear anymore.

You can remove an item from a list by using the JavaScript built-in filter functionality. The filter function takes a function as input. The function has access to each value in the list, because it iterates over the list. That way, you can evaluate each item in the list based on a filter condition. If the evaluation for an item is true, the item stays in the list. Otherwise it will be filtered from the list. Additionally, it is good to know that the function returns a new list and doesn't mutate the old list. It supports the convention in React of having immutable data structures.

Basics in React

src/App.js

```
onDismiss(id) {
  const updatedList = this.state.list.filter(function isNotId(item) {
    return item.objectID !== id;
  });
}
```

[handwritten annotation: returns all items from this.state.list that do not have an objectID matching the ID passed in]

In the next step, you can extract the function and pass it to the filter function.

src/App.js

```
onDismiss(id) {
  function isNotId(item) {
    return item.objectID !== id;
  }

  const updatedList = this.state.list.filter(isNotId);
}
```

In addition, you can do it more concisely by using a JavaScript ES6 arrow function again.

src/App.js

```
onDismiss(id) {
  const isNotId = item => item.objectID !== id;
  const updatedList = this.state.list.filter(isNotId);
}
```

You could even inline it again, like you did in the onClick handler of the button, but it might get less readable.

src/App.js

```
onDismiss(id) {
  const updatedList = this.state.list.filter(item => item.objectID !== id);
}
```

The list removes the clicked item now. However the state isn't updated yet. Therefore you can finally use the setState() class method to update the list in the internal component state.

Basics in React

src/App.js
```
onDismiss(id) {
  const isNotId = item => item.objectID !== id;
  const updatedList = this.state.list.filter(isNotId);
  this.setState({ list: updatedList });
}
```

Now run again your application and try the "Dismiss" button. It should work. What you experience now is the **unidirectional data flow** in React. You trigger an action in your view with `onClick()`, a function or class method modifies the internal component state and the `render()` method of the component runs again to update the view.

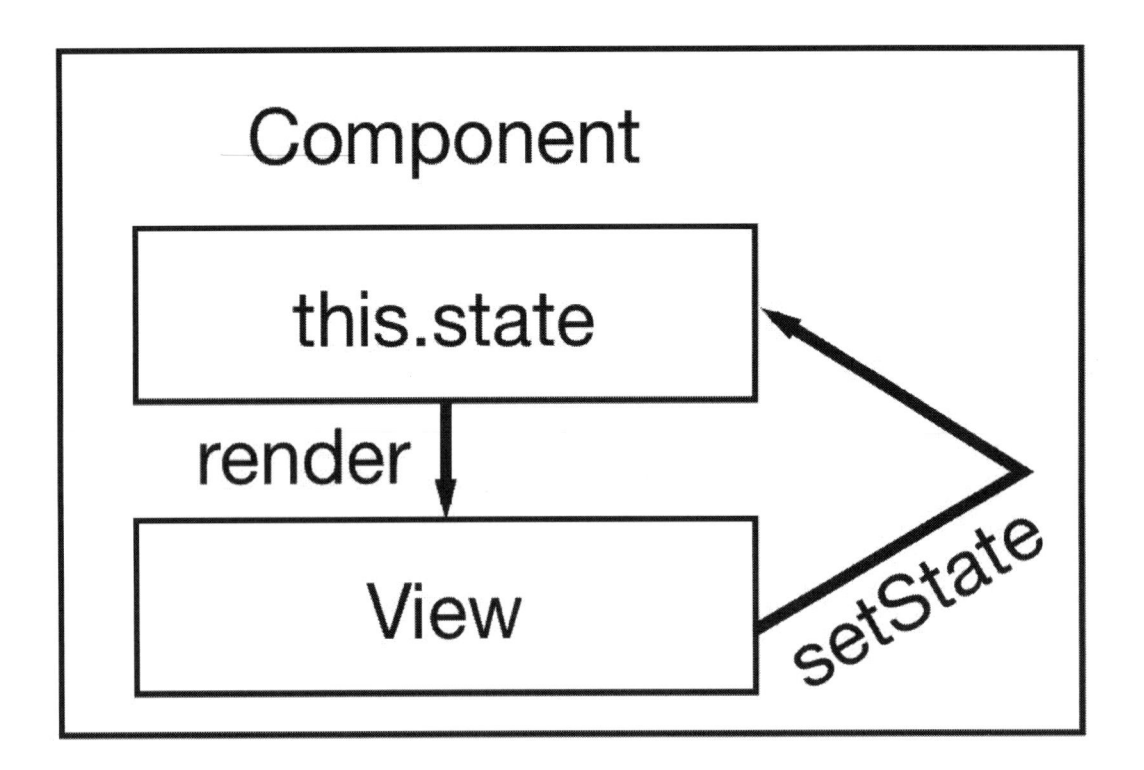

Internal state update with unidirectional data flow

Exercises:

- read more about the state and lifecycle in React[61]

---
[61]https://facebook.github.io/react/docs/state-and-lifecycle.html

Bindings

It is important to learn about bindings in JavaScript classes when using React ES6 class components. In the previous chapter, you have bound your class method onDismiss() in the constructor.

src/App.js

```
class App extends Component {
  constructor(props) {
    super(props);

    this.state = {
      list,
    };

    this.onDismiss = this.onDismiss.bind(this);
  }

  ...
}
```

Why would you do that in the first place? The binding step is necessary, because class methods don't automatically bind this to the class instance. Let's demonstrate it with the help of the following ES6 class component.

Code Playground

```
class ExplainBindingsComponent extends Component {
  onClickMe() {
    console.log(this);
  }

  render() {
    return (
      <button
        onClick={this.onClickMe}
        type="button"
      >
        Click Me
      </button>
    );
  }
}
```

Basics in React

The component renders just fine, but when you click the button, you will get `undefined` in your developer console log. That's a main source of bugs when using React, because if you want to access `this.state` in your class method, it cannot be retrieved because `this` is `undefined`. So in order to make `this` accessible in your class methods, you have to bind the class methods to `this`.

In the following class component the class method is properly bound in the class constructor.

Code Playground

```
class ExplainBindingsComponent extends Component {
  constructor() {
    super();

    this.onClickMe = this.onClickMe.bind(this);
  }

  onClickMe() {
    console.log(this);
  }

  render() {
    return (
      <button
        onClick={this.onClickMe}
        type="button"
      >
        Click Me
      </button>
    );
  }
}
```

When trying the button again, the `this` object, to be more specific the class instance, should be defined and you would be able to access `this.state`, or as you will later learn `this.props`, now.

The class method binding can happen somewhere else too. For instance, it can happen in the `render()` class method.

Basics in React

Code Playground

```
class ExplainBindingsComponent extends Component {
  onClickMe() {
    console.log(this);
  }

  render() {
    return (
      <button
        onClick={this.onClickMe.bind(this)}
        type="button"
      >
        Click Me
      </button>
    );
  }
}
```

But you should avoid it, because it would bind the class method every time when the `render()` method runs. Basically it runs every time your component updates which leads to performance implications. When binding the class method in the constructor, you bind it only once in the beginning when the component is instantiated. That's a better approach to do it.

Another thing people sometimes come up with is defining the business logic of their class methods in the constructor.

Code Playground

```
class ExplainBindingsComponent extends Component {
  constructor() {
    super();

    this.onClickMe = () => {
      console.log(this);
    }
  }

  render() {
    return (
      <button
        onClick={this.onClickMe}
        type="button"
```

```
      >
        Click Me
      </button>
    );
  }
}
```

You should avoid it too, because it will clutter your constructor over time. The constructor is only there to instantiate your class with all its properties. That's why the business logic of class methods should be defined outside of the constructor.

Code Playground

```
class ExplainBindingsComponent extends Component {
  constructor() {
    super();

    this.doSomething = this.doSomething.bind(this);
    this.doSomethingElse = this.doSomethingElse.bind(this);
  }

  doSomething() {
    // do something
  }

  doSomethingElse() {
    // do something else
  }

  ...
}
```

Last but not least, it is worth to mention that class methods can be autobound automatically without binding them explicitly by using JavaScript ES6 arrow functions.

Basics in React

Code Playground

```
class ExplainBindingsComponent extends Component {
  onClickMe = () => {
    console.log(this);
  }

  render() {
    return (
      <button
        onClick={this.onClickMe}
        type="button"
      >
        Click Me
      </button>
    );
  }
}
```

If the repetitive binding in the constructor annoys you, you can go ahead with this approach instead. The official React documentation sticks to the class method bindings in the constructor. That's why the book will stick to those as well.

Exercises:

- try the different approaches of bindings and console log the `this` object

Basics in React

Event Handler

The chapter should give you a deeper understanding of event handlers in elements. In your application, you are using the following button element to dismiss an item from the list.

src/App.js

```
...

<button
  onClick={() => this.onDismiss(item.objectID)}
  type="button"
>
  Dismiss
</button>

...
```

That's already a complex use case, because you have to pass a value to the class method and thus you have to wrap it into another (arrow) function. So basically, it has to be a function that is passed to the event handler. The following code wouldn't work, because the class method would be executed immediately when you open the application in the browser.

src/App.js

```
...

<button
  onClick={this.onDismiss(item.objectID)}
  type="button"
>
  Dismiss
</button>

...
```

When using onClick={doSomething()}, the doSomething() function would execute immediately when you open the application in your browser. The expression in the handler is evaluated. Since the returned value of the function isn't a function anymore, nothing would happen when you click the button. But when using onClick={doSomething} whereas doSomething is a function, it would be executed when clicking the button. The same rules apply for the onDismiss() class method that is used in your application.

Basics in React

However, using `onClick={this.onDismiss}` wouldn't suffice, because somehow the `item.objectID` property needs to be passed to the class method to identify the item that is going to be dismissed. That's why it can be wrapped into another function to sneak in the property. The concept is called higher order functions in JavaScript and will be explained briefly later on.

src/App.js

```
...

<button
  onClick={() => this.onDismiss(item.objectID)}
  type="button"
>
  Dismiss
</button>

...
```

A workaround would be to define the wrapping function somewhere outside and only pass the defined function to the handler. Since it needs access to the individual item, it has to live in the inside of the map function block.

src/App.js

```
class App extends Component {

  ...

  render() {
    return (
      <div className="App">
        {this.state.list.map(item => {
          const onHandleDismiss = () =>
            this.onDismiss(item.objectID);

          return (
            <div key={item.objectID}>
              <span>
                <a href={item.url}>{item.title}</a>
              </span>
              <span>{item.author}</span>
              <span>{item.num_comments}</span>
              <span>{item.points}</span>
              <span>
```

Basics in React

```
            <button
              onClick={onHandleDismiss}
              type="button"
            >
              Dismiss
            </button>
          </span>
        </div>
      );
    }
  )}
  </div>
    );
  }
}
```

After all, it has to be a function that is passed to the element's handler. As an example, try this code instead:

src/App.js

```
class App extends Component {

  ...

  render() {
    return (
      <div className="App">
        {this.state.list.map(item =>
            ...
            <span>
              <button
                onClick={console.log(item.objectID)}
                type="button"
              >
                Dismiss
              </button>
            </span>
          </div>
        )}
      </div>
    );
```

Basics in React

```
  }
}
```

It will run when you open the application in the browser but not when you click the button. Whereas the following code would only run when you click the button. It is a function that is executed when you trigger the handler.

src/App.js

```
...

<button
  onClick={function () {
    console.log(item.objectID)
  }}
  type="button"
>
  Dismiss
</button>

...
```

In order to keep it concise, you can transform it into a JavaScript ES6 arrow function again. That's what we did with the onDismiss() class method too.

src/App.js

```
...

<button
  onClick={() => console.log(item.objectID)}
  type="button"
>
  Dismiss
</button>

...
```

Often newcomers to React have difficulties with the topic of using functions in event handlers. That's why I tried to explain it in more detail here. In the end, you should end up with the following code in your button to have a concisely inlined JavaScript ES6 arrow function that has access to the objectID property of the item object.

src/App.js

```
class App extends Component {
  ...

  render() {
    return (
      <div className="App">
        {this.state.list.map(item =>
          <div key={item.objectID}>
            ...
            <span>
              <button
                onClick={() => this.onDismiss(item.objectID)}
                type="button"
              >
                Dismiss
              </button>
            </span>
          </div>
        )}
      </div>
    );
  }
}
```

Another performance relevant topic, that is often mentioned, are the implications of using arrow functions in event handlers. For instance, the onClick handler for the onDismiss() method is wrapping the method in another arrow function to be able to pass the item identifier. So every time the render() method runs, the handler instantiates the higher order arrow function. It *can* have an impact on your application performance, but in most cases you will not notice it. Imagine you have a huge table of data with 1000 items and each row or column has such an arrow function in an event handler. Then it is worth to think about the performance implications and therefore you could implement a dedicated Button component to bind the method in the constructor. But before that happens it is premature optimization. It is more valuable to focus on learning React itself.

Exercises:

- try the different approaches of using functions in the onClick handler of your button

Interactions with Forms and Events

Let's add another interaction for the application to experience forms and events in React. The interaction is a search functionality. The input of the search field should be used to filter your list temporary based on the title property of an item.

In the first step, you are going to define a form with an input field in your JSX.

src/App.js

```
class App extends Component {

  ...

  render() {
    return (
      <div className="App">
        <form>
          <input type="text" />
        </form>
        {this.state.list.map(item =>
          ...
        )}
      </div>
    );
  }
}
```

In the following scenario you will type into the input field and filter the list temporarily by the search term that is used in the input field. To be able to filter the list based on the value of the input field, you need to store the value of the input field in your local state. But how do you access the value? You can use **synthetic events** in React to access the event payload.

Let's define a `onChange` handler for the input field.

Basics in React

src/App.js

```
class App extends Component {

  ...

  render() {
    return (
      <div className="App">
        <form>
          <input
            type="text"
            onChange={this.onSearchChange}
          />
        </form>
        ...
      </div>
    );
  }
}
```

The function is bound to the component and thus a class method again. You have to bind and define the method.

src/App.js

```
class App extends Component {

  constructor(props) {
    super(props);

    this.state = {
      list,
    };

    this.onSearchChange = this.onSearchChange.bind(this);
    this.onDismiss = this.onDismiss.bind(this);
  }

  onSearchChange() {
    ...
  }
```

Basics in React

```
  ...
}
```

When using a handler in your element, you get access to the synthetic React event in your callback function's signature.

src/App.js

```
class App extends Component {

  ...

  onSearchChange(event) {
    ...
  }

  ...
}
```

The event has the value of the input field in its target object. Hence you are able to update the local state with the search term by using `this.setState()` again.

src/App.js

```
class App extends Component {

  ...

  onSearchChange(event) {
    this.setState({ searchTerm: event.target.value });
  }

  ...
}
```

Additionally, you shouldn't forget to define the initial state for the `searchTerm` property in the constructor. The input field should be empty in the beginning and thus the value should be an empty string.

Basics in React

src/App.js

```
class App extends Component {

  constructor(props) {
    super(props);

    this.state = {
      list,
      searchTerm: '',
    };

    this.onSearchChange = this.onSearchChange.bind(this);
    this.onDismiss = this.onDismiss.bind(this);
  }

  ...
}
```

Now you store the input value to your internal component state every time the value in the input field changes.

A brief note about updating the local state in a React component. It would be fair to assume that when updating the searchTerm with this.setState() the list needs to be passed as well to preserve it. But that isn't the case. React's this.setState() is a shallow merge. It preserves the sibling properties in the state object when updating one sole property in it. Thus the list state, even though you have already dismissed an item from it, would stay the same when updating the searchTerm property.

Let's get back to your application. The list isn't filtered yet based on the input field value that is stored in the local state. Basically you have to filter the list temporarily based on the searchTerm. You have everything you need to filter it. So how to filter it temporarily now? In your render() method, before you map over the list, you can apply a filter on it. The filter would only evaluate if the searchTerm matches title property of the item. You have already used the built-in JavaScript filter functionality, so let's do it again. You can sneak in the filter function before the map function, because the filter function returns a new array and thus the map function can be used on it in such a convenient way.

src/App.js

```
class App extends Component {

  ...

  render() {
    return (
      <div className="App">
        <form>
          <input
            type="text"
            onChange={this.onSearchChange}
          />
        </form>
        {this.state.list.filter(...).map(item =>
          ...
        )}
      </div>
    );
  }
}
```

Let's approach the filter function in a different way this time. We want to define the filter argument, the function that is passed to the filter function, outside of the ES6 class component. There we don't have access to the state of the component and thus we have no access to the searchTerm property to evaluate the filter condition. We have to pass the searchTerm to the filter function and have to return a new function to evaluate the condition. That's called a higher order function.

Normally I wouldn't mention higher order functions, but in a React book it makes total sense. It makes sense to know about higher order functions, because React deals with a concept called higher order components. You will get to know the concept later in the book. Now again, let's focus on the filter functionality.

First, you have to define the higher order function outside of your App component.

src/App.js
```
function isSearched(searchTerm) {
  return function(item) {
    // some condition which returns true or false
  }
}

class App extends Component {

  ...

}
```

The function takes the `searchTerm` and returns another function, because after all the filter function takes a function as its input. The returned function has access to the item object because it is the function that is passed to the filter function. In addition, the returned function will be used to filter the list based on the condition defined in the function. Let's define the condition.

src/App.js
```
function isSearched(searchTerm) {
  return function(item) {
    return item.title.toLowerCase().includes(searchTerm.toLowerCase());
  }
}

class App extends Component {

  ...

}
```

The condition says that you match the incoming `searchTerm` pattern with the title property of the item from your list. You can do that with the built-in `includes` JavaScript functionality. Only when the pattern matches, you return true and the item stays in the list. When the pattern doesn't match the item is removed from the list. But be careful with pattern matching: You shouldn't forget to lower case both strings. Otherwise there will be mismatches between a search term 'redux' and an item title 'Redux'. Since we are working on a immutable list and return a new list by using the filter function, the original list in the local state isn't modified at all.

One thing is left to mention: We cheated a bit by using the built-in includes JavaScript functionality. It is already an ES6 feature. How would that look like in JavaScript ES5? You would use the `indexOf()` function to get the index of the item in the list. When the item is in the list, `indexOf()` will return its index in the array.

Basics in React

Code Playground

```
// ES5
string.indexOf(pattern) !== -1

// ES6
string.includes(pattern)
```

Another neat refactoring can be done with an ES6 arrow function again. It makes the function more concise:

Code Playground

```
// ES5
function isSearched(searchTerm) {
  return function(item) {
    return item.title.toLowerCase().includes(searchTerm.toLowerCase());
  }
}

// ES6
const isSearched = searchTerm => item =>
  item.title.toLowerCase().includes(searchTerm.toLowerCase());
```

One could argue which function is more readable. Personally I prefer the second one. The React ecosystem uses a lot of functional programming concepts. It happens often that you will use a function which returns a function (higher order functions). In JavaScript ES6, you can express these more concisely with arrow functions.

Last but not least, you have to use the defined `isSearched()` function to filter your list. You pass it the `searchTerm` property from your local state, it returns the filter input function, and filters your list based on the filter condition. Afterward it maps over the filtered list to display an element for each list item.

Basics in React

src/App.js

```
class App extends Component {

  ...

  render() {
    return (
      <div className="App">
        <form>
          <input
            type="text"
            onChange={this.onSearchChange}
          />
        </form>
        {this.state.list.filter(isSearched(this.state.searchTerm)).map(item =>
          ...
        )}
      </div>
    );
  }
}
```

The search functionality should work now. Try it yourself in the browser.

Exercises:

- read more about React events[62]
- read more about higher order functions[63]

---

[62]https://facebook.github.io/react/docs/handling-events.html
[63]https://en.wikipedia.org/wiki/Higher-order_function

ES6 Destructuring

There is a way in JavaScript ES6 for an easier access to properties in objects and arrays. It's called destructuring. Compare the following snippet in JavaScript ES5 and ES6.

Code Playground

```
const user = {
  firstname: 'Robin',
  lastname: 'Wieruch',
};

// ES5
var firstname = user.firstname;
var lastname = user.lastname;

console.log(firstname + ' ' + lastname);
// output: Robin Wieruch

// ES6
const { firstname, lastname } = user;

console.log(firstname + ' ' + lastname);
// output: Robin Wieruch
```

While you have to add an extra line each time you want to access an object property in JavaScript ES5, you can do it in one line in JavaScript ES6. A best practice for readability is to use multilines when you destructure an object into multiple properties.

Code Playground

```
const {
  firstname,
  lastname
} = user;
```

The same goes for arrays. You can destructure them too. Again, multilines will keep your code scannable and readable.

Basics in React

Code Playground
```
const users = ['Robin', 'Andrew', 'Dan'];
const [
  userOne,
  userTwo,
  userThree
] = users;

console.log(userOne, userTwo, userThree);
// output: Robin Andrew Dan
```

Perhaps you have noticed that the local state object in the App component can get destructured the same way. You can shorten the filter and map line of code.

src/App.js
```
render() {
  const { searchTerm, list } = this.state;
  return (
    <div className="App">
      ...
      {list.filter(isSearched(searchTerm)).map(item =>
        ...
      )}
    </div>
  );
```

You can do it the ES5 or ES6 way:

Code Playground
```
// ES5
var searchTerm = this.state.searchTerm;
var list = this.state.list;

// ES6
const { searchTerm, list } = this.state;
```

But since the book uses JavaScript ES6 most of the time, you should stick to it.

Exercises:

- read more about ES6 destructuring[64]

---

[64] https://developer.mozilla.org/en/docs/Web/JavaScript/Reference/Operators/Destructuring_assignment

Controlled Components

You already learned about the unidirectional data flow in React. The same law applies for the input field, which updates the local state with the searchTerm in order to filter the list. When the state changes, the render() method runs again and uses the recent searchTerm from the local state to apply the filter condition.

But didn't we forget something in the input element? A HTML input tag comes with a value attribute. The value attribute usually has the value that is shown in the input field. In this case it would be the searchTerm property. However, it seems like we don't need that in React.

That's wrong. Form elements such as <input>, <textarea> and <select> hold their own state in plain HTML. They modify the value internally once someone changes it from the outside. In React that's called an **uncontrolled component**, because it handles its own state. In React, you should make sure to make those elements **controlled components**.

How should you do that? You only have to set the value attribute of the input field. The value is already saved in the searchTerm state property. So why not access it from there?

src/App.js

```
class App extends Component {

  ...

  render() {
    const { searchTerm, list } = this.state;
    return (
      <div className="App">
        <form>
          <input
            type="text"
            value={searchTerm}
            onChange={this.onSearchChange}
          />
        </form>
        ...
      </div>
    );
  }
}
```

That's it. The unidirectional data flow loop for the input field is self-contained now. The internal component state is the single source of truth for the input field.

The whole internal state management and unidirectional data flow might be new to you. But once you are used to it, it will be your natural flow to implement things in React. In general, React brought a novel pattern with the unidirectional data flow to the world of single page applications. It is adopted by several frameworks and libraries by now.

Exercises:

- read more about React forms[65]

---

[65] https://facebook.github.io/react/docs/forms.html

Split Up Components

You have one large App component now. It keeps growing and can become confusing eventually. You can start to split it up into chunks of smaller components.

Let's start to use a component for the search input and a component for the list of items.

src/App.js

```
class App extends Component {

  ...

  render() {
    const { searchTerm, list } = this.state;
    return (
      <div className="App">
        <Search />
        <Table />
      </div>
    );
  }
}
```

You can pass those components properties which they can use themselves. In the case of the App component it needs to pass the properties managed in the local state and its class methods.

src/App.js

```
class App extends Component {

  ...

  render() {
    const { searchTerm, list } = this.state;
    return (
      <div className="App">
        <Search
          value={searchTerm}
          onChange={this.onSearchChange}
        />
        <Table
          list={list}
```

```
          pattern={searchTerm}
          onDismiss={this.onDismiss}
        />
      </div>
    );
  }
}
```

Now you can define the components next to your App component. Those components will be ES6 class components as well. They render the same elements like before.

The first one is the Search component.

src/App.js

```
class App extends Component {
  ...
}

class Search extends Component {
  render() {
    const { value, onChange } = this.props;
    return (
      <form>
        <input
          type="text"
          value={value}
          onChange={onChange}
        />
      </form>
    );
  }
}
```

The second one is the Table component.

src/App.js

```
...

class Table extends Component {
  render() {
    const { list, pattern, onDismiss } = this.props;
    return (
      <div>
        {list.filter(isSearched(pattern)).map(item =>
          <div key={item.objectID}>
            <span>
              <a href={item.url}>{item.title}</a>
            </span>
            <span>{item.author}</span>
            <span>{item.num_comments}</span>
            <span>{item.points}</span>
            <span>
              <button
                onClick={() => onDismiss(item.objectID)}
                type="button"
              >
                Dismiss
              </button>
            </span>
          </div>
        )}
      </div>
    );
  }
}
```

Now you have three ES6 class components. Perhaps you have noticed the props object that is accessible via the class instance by using this. The props, short form for properties, have all the values you have passed to the components when you used them in your App component. That way, components can pass properties down the component tree.

By extracting those components from the App component, you would be able to reuse them somewhere else. Since components get their values by using the props object, you can pass every time different props to your components when you use them somewhere else. These components became reusable.

Exercises:

- figure out further components that you could split up as you have done with the Search and Table components
    - but don't do it now, otherwise you will run into conflicts in the next chapters

Composable Components

There is one more little property which is accessible in the props object: the `children` prop. You can use it to pass elements to your components from above, which are unknown to the component itself, but make it possible to compose components into each other. Let's see how this looks like when you only pass a text (string) as a child to the Search component.

src/App.js

```
class App extends Component {

  ...

  render() {
    const { searchTerm, list } = this.state;
    return (
      <div className="App">
        <Search
          value={searchTerm}
          onChange={this.onSearchChange}
        >
          Search
        </Search>
        <Table
          list={list}
          pattern={searchTerm}
          onDismiss={this.onDismiss}
        />
      </div>
    );
  }
}
```

Now the Search component can destructure the children property from the props object. Then it can specify where the children should be displayed.

src/App.js

```
class Search extends Component {
  render() {
    const { value, onChange, children } = this.props;
    return (
      <form>
        {children} <input
          type="text"
          value={value}
          onChange={onChange}
        />
      </form>
    );
  }
}
```

The "Search" text should be visible next to your input field now. When you use the Search component somewhere else, you can choose a different text if you like. After all, it is not only text that you can pass as children. You can pass an element and element trees (which can be encapsulated by components again) as children. The children property makes it possible to weave components into each other.

Exercises:

- read more about the composition model of React[66]

---

[66] https://facebook.github.io/react/docs/composition-vs-inheritance.html

Reusable Components

Reusable and composable components empower you to come up with capable component hierarchies. They are the foundation of React's view layer. The last chapters mentioned the term reusability. You can reuse the Table and Search components by now. Even the App component is reusable, because you could instantiate it somewhere else again.

Let's define one more reusable component, a Button component, which gets reused more often eventually.

src/App.js

```
class Button extends Component {
  render() {
    const {
      onClick,
      className,
      children,
    } = this.props;

    return (
      <button
        onClick={onClick}
        className={className}
        type="button"
      >
        {children}
      </button>
    );
  }
}
```

It might seem redundant to declare such a component. You will use a Button component instead of a button element. It only spares the type="button". Except for the type attribute you have to define everything else when you want to use the Button component. But you have to think about the long term investment here. Imagine you have several buttons in your application, but want to change an attribute, style or behavior for the button. Without the component you would have to refactor every button. Instead the Button component ensures to have only one single source of truth. One Button to refactor all buttons at once. One Button to rule them all.

Since you already have a button element, you can use the Button component instead. It omits the type attribute, because the Button component specifies it.

src/App.js

```
class Table extends Component {
  render() {
    const { list, pattern, onDismiss } = this.props;
    return (
      <div>
        {list.filter(isSearched(pattern)).map(item =>
          <div key={item.objectID}>
            <span>
              <a href={item.url}>{item.title}</a>
            </span>
            <span>{item.author}</span>
            <span>{item.num_comments}</span>
            <span>{item.points}</span>
            <span>
              <Button onClick={() => onDismiss(item.objectID)}>
                Dismiss
              </Button>
            </span>
          </div>
        )}
      </div>
    );
  }
}
```

The Button component expects a `className` property in the props. The `className` attribute is another React derivate for the HTML attribute class. But we didn't pass any `className` when the Button was used. In the code it should be more explicit in the Button component that the `className` is optional.

Therefore, you can use the default parameter which is a JavaScript ES6 feature.

src/App.js

```
class Button extends Component {
  render() {
    const {
      onClick,
      className = '',
      children,
    } = this.props;

    ...
  }
}
```

Now, whenever there is no `className` property specified when using the Button component, the value will be an empty string instead of `undefined`.

Exercises:

- read more about ES6 default parameters[67]

---

[67] https://developer.mozilla.org/en/docs/Web/JavaScript/Reference/Functions/Default_parameters

Component Declarations

By now you have four ES6 class components. But you can do better. Let me introduce functional stateless components as alternative for ES6 class components. Before you will refactor your components, let's introduce the different types of components in React.

- **Functional Stateless Components**: These components are functions which get an input and return an output. The input are the props. The output is a component instance thus plain JSX. So far it is quite similar to an ES6 class component. However, functional stateless components are functions (functional) and they have no local state (stateless). You cannot access or update the state with `this.state` or `this.setState()` because there is no `this` object. Additionally, they have no lifecycle methods. You didn't learn about lifecycle methods yet, but you already used two: `constructor()` and `render()`. Whereas the constructor runs only once in the lifetime of a component, the `render()` class method runs once in the beginning and every time the component updates. Keep in mind that functional stateless component have no lifecycle methods, when you arrive at the lifecycle methods chapter later on.
- **ES6 Class Components**: You already used this type of component declaration in your four components. In the class definition, they extend from the React component. The extend hooks all the lifecycle methods, available in the React component API, to the component. That way you were able to use the `render()` class method. Additionally, you can store and manipulate state in ES6 class components by using `this.state` and `this.setState()`.
- **React.createClass**: The component declaration was used in older versions of React and still in JavaScript ES5 React applications. But Facebook declared it as deprecated[68] in favor of JavaScript ES6. They even added a deprecation warning in version 15.5[69]. You will not use it in the book.

So basically there are only two component declarations left. But when to use functional stateless components over ES6 class components? A rule of thumb is to use functional stateless components when you don't need local state or component lifecycle methods. Usually you start to implement your components as functional stateless components. Once you need access to the state or lifecycle methods, you have to refactor it to an ES6 class component. In our application, we started the other way around for the sake of learning React.

Let's get back to your application. The App component uses internal state. That's why it has to stay as an ES6 class component. But the other three of your ES6 class components are stateless. They don't need access to `this.state` or `this.setState()`. Even more, they have no lifecycle methods. Let's refactor together the Search component to a stateless functional component. The Table and Button component refactoring will remain as your exercise.

---

[68] https://facebook.github.io/react/blog/2015/03/10/react-v0.13.html
[69] https://facebook.github.io/react/blog/2017/04/07/react-v15.5.0.html

Basics in React

src/App.js

```
function Search(props) {
  const { value, onChange, children } = props;
  return (
    <form>
      {children} <input
        type="text"
        value={value}
        onChange={onChange}
      />
    </form>
  );
}
```

That's basically it. The props are accessible in the function signature and the return value is JSX. But you can do more code wise in a functional stateless component. You already know the ES6 destructuring. The best practice is to use it in the function signature to destructure the props.

src/App.js

```
function Search({ value, onChange, children }) {
  return (
    <form>
      {children} <input
        type="text"
        value={value}
        onChange={onChange}
      />
    </form>
  );
}
```

But it can get better. You know already that ES6 arrow functions allow you to keep your functions concise. You can remove the block body of the function. In a concise body an implicit return is attached thus you can remove the return statement. Since your functional stateless component is a function, you can keep it concise as well.

Basics in React

src/App.js
```
const Search = ({ value, onChange, children }) =>
  <form>
    {children} <input
      type="text"
      value={value}
      onChange={onChange}
    />
  </form>
```

The last step was especially useful to enforce only to have props as input and JSX as output. Nothing in between. Still, you could *do something* in between by using a block body in your ES6 arrow function.

Code Playground

```
const Search = ({ value, onChange, children }) => {

  // do something

  return (
    <form>
      {children} <input
        type="text"
        value={value}
        onChange={onChange}
      />
    </form>
  );
}
```

But you don't need it for now. That's why you can keep the previous version without the block body. When using block bodies, people often tend to do too many things in the function. By leaving the block body out, you can focus on the input and output of your function.

Now you have one lightweight functional stateless component. Once you would need access to its internal component state or lifecycle methods, you would refactor it to an ES6 class component. In addition you saw how JavaScript ES6 can be used in React components to make them more concise and elegant.

Exercises:

- refactor the Table and Button component to stateless functional components
- read more about ES6 class components and functional stateless components[70]

---

[70] https://facebook.github.io/react/docs/components-and-props.html

Styling Components

Let's add some basic styling to your application and components. You can reuse the *src/App.css* and *src/index.css* files. These files should already be in your project since you have bootstrapped it with *create-react-app*. They should be imported in your *src/App.js* and *src/index.js* files too. I prepared some CSS which you can simply copy and paste to these files, but feel free to use your own style at this point.

First, styling for your overall application.

src/index.css

```css
body {
  color: #222;
  background: #f4f4f4;
  font: 400 14px CoreSans, Arial,sans-serif;
}

a {
  color: #222;
}

a:hover {
  text-decoration: underline;
}

ul, li {
  list-style: none;
  padding: 0;
  margin: 0;
}

input {
  padding: 10px;
  border-radius: 5px;
  outline: none;
  margin-right: 10px;
  border: 1px solid #dddddd;
}

button {
  padding: 10px;
  border-radius: 5px;
```

Basics in React

```css
  border: 1px solid #dddddd;
  background: transparent;
  color: #808080;
  cursor: pointer;
}

button:hover {
  color: #222;
}

*:focus {
  outline: none;
}
```

Second, styling for your components in the App file.

src/App.css

```css
.page {
  margin: 20px;
}

.interactions {
  text-align: center;
}

.table {
  margin: 20px 0;
}

.table-header {
  display: flex;
  line-height: 24px;
  font-size: 16px;
  padding: 0 10px;
  justify-content: space-between;
}

.table-empty {
  margin: 200px;
  text-align: center;
  font-size: 16px;
}
```

```css
.table-row {
  display: flex;
  line-height: 24px;
  white-space: nowrap;
  margin: 10px 0;
  padding: 10px;
  background: #ffffff;
  border: 1px solid #e3e3e3;
}

.table-header > span {
  overflow: hidden;
  text-overflow: ellipsis;
  padding: 0 5px;
}

.table-row > span {
  overflow: hidden;
  text-overflow: ellipsis;
  padding: 0 5px;
}

.button-inline {
  border-width: 0;
  background: transparent;
  color: inherit;
  text-align: inherit;
  -webkit-font-smoothing: inherit;
  padding: 0;
  font-size: inherit;
  cursor: pointer;
}

.button-active {
  border-radius: 0;
  border-bottom: 1px solid #38BB6C;
}
```

Now you can use the style in some of your components. Don't forget to use React `className` instead of `class` as HTML attribute.

First, apply it in your App ES6 class component.

Basics in React

src/App.js

```
class App extends Component {

  ...

  render() {
    const { searchTerm, list } = this.state;
    return (
      <div className="page">
        <div className="interactions">
          <Search
            value={searchTerm}
            onChange={this.onSearchChange}
          >
            Search
          </Search>
        </div>
        <Table
          list={list}
          pattern={searchTerm}
          onDismiss={this.onDismiss}
        />
      </div>
    );
  }
}
```

Second, apply it in your Table functional stateless component.

src/App.js

```
const Table = ({ list, pattern, onDismiss }) =>
  <div className="table">
    {list.filter(isSearched(pattern)).map(item =>
      <div key={item.objectID} className="table-row">
        <span>
          <a href={item.url}>{item.title}</a>
        </span>
        <span>{item.author}</span>
        <span>{item.num_comments}</span>
        <span>{item.points}</span>
        <span>
```

```
      <Button
        onClick={() => onDismiss(item.objectID)}
        className="button-inline"
      >
        Dismiss
      </Button>
    </span>
  </div>
  )}
</div>
```

Now you have styled your application and components with basic CSS. It should look quite decent. As you know, JSX mixes up HTML and JavaScript. Now one could argue to add CSS in the mix as well. That's called inline style. You can define JavaScript objects and pass them to the style attribute of an element.

Let's keep the Table column width flexible by using inline style.

src/App.js

```
const Table = ({ list, pattern, onDismiss }) =>
  <div className="table">
    {list.filter(isSearched(pattern)).map(item =>
      <div key={item.objectID} className="table-row">
        <span style={{ width: '40%' }}>
          <a href={item.url}>{item.title}</a>
        </span>
        <span style={{ width: '30%' }}>
          {item.author}
        </span>
        <span style={{ width: '10%' }}>
          {item.num_comments}
        </span>
        <span style={{ width: '10%' }}>
          {item.points}
        </span>
        <span style={{ width: '10%' }}>
          <Button
            onClick={() => onDismiss(item.objectID)}
            className="button-inline"
          >
            Dismiss
          </Button>
```

```
      </span>
    </div>
  )}
</div>
```

The style is inlined now. You could define the style objects outside of your elements to make it cleaner.

Code Playground

```
const largeColumn = {
  width: '40%',
};

const midColumn = {
  width: '30%',
};

const smallColumn = {
  width: '10%',
};
```

After that you would use them in your columns: `<span style={smallColumn}>`.

In general, you will find different opinions and solutions for style in React. You used pure CSS and inline style now. That's sufficient to get started.

I don't want to be opinionated here, but I want to leave you some more options. You can read about them and apply them on your own. But if you are new to React, I would recommend to stick to pure CSS and inline style for now.

- styled-components[71]
- CSS Modules[72]

---

[71]https://github.com/styled-components/styled-components
[72]https://github.com/css-modules/css-modules

Basics in React

You have learned the basics to write your own React application! Let's recap the last chapters:

- React
    - use `this.state` and `setState()` to manage your internal component state
    - pass functions or class methods to your element handler
    - use forms and events in React to add interactions
    - unidirectional data flow is an important concept in React
    - embrace controlled components
    - compose components with children and reusable components
    - usage and implementation of ES6 class components and functional stateless components
    - approaches to style your components
- ES6
    - functions that are bound to a class are class methods
    - destructuring of objects and arrays
    - default parameters
- General
    - higher order functions

Again it makes sense to take a break. Internalize the learnings and apply them on your own. You can experiment with the source code you have written so far. Additionally you can read more in the official documentation[73].

You can find the source code in the official repository[74].

---

[73] https://facebook.github.io/react/docs/installation.html
[74] https://github.com/rwieruch/hackernews-client/tree/4.2

Getting Real with an API

Now it's time to get real with an API, because it can get boring to deal with sample data.

If you are not familiar with APIs, I encourage you to read my journey where I got to know APIs[75].

Do you know the Hacker News[76] platform? It's a great news aggregator about tech topics. In this book, you will use the Hacker News API to fetch trending stories from the platform. There is a basic[77] and search[78] API to get data from the platform. The latter one makes sense in the case of this application in order to search stories on Hacker News. You can visit the API specification to get an understanding of the data structure.

---

[75] https://www.robinwieruch.de/what-is-an-api-javascript/
[76] https://news.ycombinator.com/
[77] https://github.com/HackerNews/API
[78] https://hn.algolia.com/api

Lifecycle Methods

You will need to know about React lifecycle methods before you can start to fetch data in your components by using an API. These methods are a hook into the lifecycle of a React component. They can be used in ES6 class components, but not in functional stateless components.

Do you remember when a previous chapter taught you about JavaScript ES6 classes and how they are used in React? Apart from the render() method, there are several methods that can be overridden in a React ES6 class component. All of these are the lifecycle methods. Let's dive into them:

You already know two lifecycle methods that can be used in an ES6 class component: constructor() and render().

The constructor is only called when an instance of the component is created and inserted in the DOM. The component gets instantiated. That process is called mounting of the component.

The render() method is called during the mount process too, but also when the component updates. Each time when the state or the props of a component change, the render() method of the component is called.

Now you know more about the two lifecycle methods and when they are called. You already used them as well. But there are more of them.

The mounting of a component has two more lifecycle methods: componentWillMount() and componentDidMount(). The constructor is called first, componentWillMount() gets called before the render() method and componentDidMount() is called after the render() method.

Overall the mounting process has 4 lifecycle methods. They are invoked in the following order:

- constructor()
- componentWillMount()
- render()
- componentDidMount()

But what about the update lifecycle of a component that happens when the state or the props change? Overall it has 5 lifecycle methods in the following order:

- componentWillReceiveProps()
- shouldComponentUpdate()
- componentWillUpdate()
- render()
- componentDidUpdate()

Getting Real with an API 83

Last but not least there is the unmounting lifecycle. It has only one lifecycle method: `componentWillUnmount()`.

After all, you don't need to know all of these lifecycle methods from the beginning. It can be intimidating yet you will not use all of them. Even in a larger React application you will only use a few of them apart from the `constructor()` and the `render()` method. Still, it is good to know that each lifecycle method can be used for specific use cases:

- **constructor(props)** - It is called when the component gets initialized. You can set an initial component state and bind class methods during that lifecycle method.
- **componentWillMount()** - It is called before the `render()` lifecycle method. That's why it could be used to set internal component state, because it will not trigger a second rendering of the component. Generally it is recommended to use the `constructor()` to set the initial state.
- **render()** - The lifecycle method is mandatory and returns the elements as an output of the component. The method should be pure and therefore shouldn't modify the component state. It gets an input as props and state and returns an element.
- **componentDidMount()** - It is called only once when the component mounted. That's the perfect time to do an asynchronous request to fetch data from an API. The fetched data would get stored in the internal component state to display it in the `render()` lifecycle method.
- **componentWillReceiveProps(nextProps)** - The lifecycle method is called during an update lifecycle. As input you get the next props. You can diff the next props with the previous props, by using `this.props`, to apply a different behavior based on the diff. Additionally, you can set state based on the next props.
- **shouldComponentUpdate(nextProps, nextState)** - It is always called when the component updates due to state or props changes. You will use it in mature React applications for performance optimizations. Depending on a boolean that you return from this lifecycle method, the component and all its children will render or will not render on an update lifecycle. You can prevent the render lifecycle method of a component.
- **componentWillUpdate(nextProps, nextState)** - The lifecycle method is immediately invoked before the `render()` method. You already have the next props and next state at your disposal. You can use the method as last opportunity to perform preparations before the render method gets executed. Note that you cannot trigger `setState()` anymore. If you want to compute state based on the next props, you have to use `componentWillReceiveProps()`.
- **componentDidUpdate(prevProps, prevState)** - The lifecycle method is immediately invoked after the `render()` method. You can use it as opportunity to perform DOM operations or to perform further asynchronous requests.
- **componentWillUnmount()** - It is called before you destroy your component. You can use the lifecycle method to perform any clean up tasks.

The `constructor()` and `render()` lifecycle methods are already used by you. These are the commonly used lifecycle methods for ES6 class components. Actually the `render()` method is required, otherwise you wouldn't return a component instance.

There is one more lifecycle method: componentDidCatch(error, info). It was introduced in React 16[79] and is used to catch errors in components. For instance, displaying the sample list in your application works just fine. But there could be a case when the list in the local state is set to null by accident (e.g. when fetching the list from an external API, but the request failed and you set the local state of the list to null). Afterward, it wouldn't be possible to filter and map the list anymore, because it is null and not an empty list. The component would be broken and the whole application would fail. Now, by using componentDidCatch(), you can catch the error, store it in your local state, and show an optional message to your application user that an error has happened.

Exercises:

- read more about lifecycle methods in React[80]
- read more about the state related to lifecycle methods in React[81]
- read more about error handling in components[82]

---

[79] https://www.robinwieruch.de/what-is-new-in-react-16/
[80] https://facebook.github.io/react/docs/react-component.html
[81] https://facebook.github.io/react/docs/state-and-lifecycle.html
[82] https://reactjs.org/blog/2017/07/26/error-handling-in-react-16.html

Fetching Data

Now you are prepared to fetch data from the Hacker News API. There was one lifecycle method mentioned that can be used to fetch data: `componentDidMount()`. You will use the native fetch API in JavaScript to perform the request.

Before we can use it, let's set up the URL constants and default parameters to breakup the API request into chunks.

src/App.js

```
import React, { Component } from 'react';
import './App.css';

const DEFAULT_QUERY = 'redux';

const PATH_BASE = 'https://hn.algolia.com/api/v1';
const PATH_SEARCH = '/search';
const PARAM_SEARCH = 'query=';

...
```

In JavaScript ES6, you can use template strings[83] to concatenate strings. You will use it to concatenate your URL for the API endpoint.

Code Playground

```
// ES6
const url = `${PATH_BASE}${PATH_SEARCH}?${PARAM_SEARCH}${DEFAULT_QUERY}`;

// ES5
var url = PATH_BASE + PATH_SEARCH + '?' + PARAM_SEARCH + DEFAULT_QUERY;

console.log(url);
// output: https://hn.algolia.com/api/v1/search?query=redux
```

That will keep your URL composition flexible in the future.

But let's get to the API request where you will use the url. The whole data fetch process will be presented at once, but each step will be explained afterward.

---

[83] https://developer.mozilla.org/en/docs/Web/JavaScript/Reference/Template_literals

Getting Real with an API

src/App.js

```
...

class App extends Component {

  constructor(props) {
    super(props);

    this.state = {
      result: null,
      searchTerm: DEFAULT_QUERY,
    };

    this.setSearchTopStories = this.setSearchTopStories.bind(this);
    this.fetchSearchTopStories = this.fetchSearchTopStories.bind(this);
    this.onSearchChange = this.onSearchChange.bind(this);
    this.onDismiss = this.onDismiss.bind(this);
  }

  setSearchTopStories(result) {
    this.setState({ result });
  }

  fetchSearchTopStories(searchTerm) {
    fetch(`${PATH_BASE}${PATH_SEARCH}?${PARAM_SEARCH}${searchTerm}`)
      .then(response => response.json())
      .then(result => this.setSearchTopStories(result))
      .catch(e => e);
  }

  componentDidMount() {
    const { searchTerm } = this.state;
    this.fetchSearchTopStories(searchTerm);
  }

  ...
}
```

A lot of things happen in the code. I thought about breaking it into smaller pieces. Then again it would be difficult to grasp the relations of each piece to each other. Let me explain each step in detail.

Getting Real with an API

First, you can remove the sample list of items, because you return a real list from the Hacker News API. The sample data is not used anymore. The initial state of your component has an empty result and default search term now. The same default search term is used in the input field of the Search component and in your first request.

Second, you use the componentDidMount() lifecycle method to fetch the data after the component did mount. In the very first fetch, the default search term from the local state is used. It will fetch "redux" related stories, because that is the default parameter.

Third, the native fetch API is used. The JavaScript ES6 template strings allow it to compose the URL with the searchTerm. The URL is the argument for the native fetch API function. The response needs to get transformed to a JSON data structure, which is a mandatory step in a native fetch function when dealing with JSON data structures, and can finally be set as result in the internal component state. In addition, the catch block is used in case of an error. If an error happens during the request, the function will run into the catch block instead of the then block. In a later chapter of the book, you will include the error handling.

Last but not least, don't forget to bind your new component methods in the constructor.

Now you can use the fetched data instead of the sample list of items. However, you have to be careful again. The result is not only a list of data. It's a complex object with meta information and a list of hits which are in our case the stories[84]. You can output the internal state with console.log(this.state); in your render() method to visualize it.

In the next step, you will use the result to render it. But we will prevent it from rendering anything, so we will return null, when there is no result in the first place. Once the request to the API succeeded, the result is saved to the state and the App component will re-render with the updated state.

src/App.js

```
class App extends Component {

  ...

  render() {
    const { searchTerm, result } = this.state;

    if (!result) { return null; }

    return (
      <div className="page">
        ...
        <Table
          list={result.hits}
          pattern={searchTerm}
```

[84]https://hn.algolia.com/api

```
            onDismiss={this.onDismiss}
          />
        </div>
      );
    }
  }
```

Let's recap what happens during the component lifecycle. Your component gets initialized by the constructor. After that, it renders for the first time. But you prevent it from displaying anything, because the result in the local state is null. It is allowed to return null for a component in order to display nothing. Then the `componentDidMount()` lifecycle method runs. In that method you fetch the data from the Hacker News API asynchronously. Once the data arrives, it changes your internal component state in `setSearchTopStories()`. Afterward, the update lifecycle comes into play because the local state was updated. The component runs the `render()` method again, but this time with populated result in your internal component state. The component and thus the Table component with its content will be rendered.

You used the native fetch API that is supported by most browsers to perform an asynchronous request to an API. The *create-react-app* configuration makes sure that it is supported in every browser. There are third-party node packages that you can use to substitute the native fetch API: superagent[85] and axios[86].

Back to your application: The list of hits should be visible now. However, there are two regression bugs in the application now. First, the "Dismiss" button is broken. It doesn't know about the complex result object and still operates on the plain list from the local state when dismissing an item. Second, when the list is displayed but you try to search for something else, the list gets filtered on the client-side even though the initial search was made by searching for stories on the server-side. The perfect behvaior would be to fetch another result object from the API when using the Search component. Both regression bugs will be fixed in the following chapters.

Exercises:

- read more about ES6 template strings[87]
- read more about the native fetch API[88]
- read more about data fetching in React[89]

---

[85] https://github.com/visionmedia/superagent
[86] https://github.com/mzabriskie/axios
[87] https://developer.mozilla.org/en/docs/Web/JavaScript/Reference/Template_literals
[88] https://developer.mozilla.org/en/docs/Web/API/Fetch_API
[89] https://www.robinwieruch.de/react-fetching-data/

ES6 Spread Operators

The "Dismiss" button doesn't work because the `onDismiss()` method is not aware of the complex result object. It only knows about a plain list in the local state. But it isn't a plain list anymore. Let's change it to operate on the result object instead of the list itself.

src/App.js

```
onDismiss(id) {
  const isNotId = item => item.objectID !== id;
  const updatedHits = this.state.result.hits.filter(isNotId);
  this.setState({
    ...
  });
}
```

But what happens in `setState()` now? Unfortunately the result is a complex object. The list of hits is only one of multiple properties in the object. However, only the list gets updated, when an item gets removed in the result object, while the other properties stay the same.

One approach could be to mutate the hits in the result object. I will demonstrate it, but we won't do it that way.

Code Playground

```
// don`t do this
this.state.result.hits = updatedHits;
```

React embraces immutable data structures. Thus you shouldn't mutate an object (or mutate the state directly). A better approach is to generate a new object based on the information you have. Thereby none of the objects get altered. You will keep the immutable data structures. You will always return a new object and never alter an object.

Therefore you can use JavaScript ES6 `Object.assign()`. It takes as first argument a target object. All following arguments are source objects. These objects are merged into the target object. The target object can be an empty object. It embraces immutability, because no source object gets mutated. It would look similar to the following:

Code Playground

```
const updatedHits = { hits: updatedHits };
const updatedResult = Object.assign({}, this.state.result, updatedHits);
```

Latter objects will override former merged objects when they share the same property names. Now let's do it in the `onDismiss()` method:

Getting Real with an API

src/App.js

```
onDismiss(id) {
  const isNotId = item => item.objectID !== id;
  const updatedHits = this.state.result.hits.filter(isNotId);
  this.setState({
    result: Object.assign({}, this.state.result, { hits: updatedHits })
  });
}
```

That would already be the solution. But there is a simpler way in JavaScript ES6 and future JavaScript releases. May I introduce the spread operator to you? It only consists of three dots: ... When it is used, every value from an array or object gets copied to another array or object.

Let's examine the ES6 **array** spread operator even though you don't need it yet.

Code Playground

```
const userList = ['Robin', 'Andrew', 'Dan'];
const additionalUser = 'Jordan';
const allUsers = [ ...userList, additionalUser ];

console.log(allUsers);
// output: ['Robin', 'Andrew', 'Dan', 'Jordan']
```

The `allUsers` variable is a completely new array. The other variables `userList` and `additionalUser` stay the same. You can even merge two arrays that way into a new array.

Code Playground

```
const oldUsers = ['Robin', 'Andrew'];
const newUsers = ['Dan', 'Jordan'];
const allUsers = [ ...oldUsers, ...newUsers ];

console.log(allUsers);
// output: ['Robin', 'Andrew', 'Dan', 'Jordan']
```

Now let's have a look at the object spread operator. It is not JavaScript ES6. It is a proposal for a next JavaScript version[90] yet already used by the React community. That's why *create-react-app* incorporated the feature in the configuration.

Basically it is the same as the JavaScript ES6 array spread operator but with objects. It copies each key value pair into a new object.

[90] https://github.com/sebmarkbage/ecmascript-rest-spread

Getting Real with an API

Code Playground

```
const userNames = { firstname: 'Robin', lastname: 'Wieruch' };
const age = 28;
const user = { ...userNames, age };

console.log(user);
// output: { firstname: 'Robin', lastname: 'Wieruch', age: 28 }
```

Multiple objects can be spread like in the array spread example.

Code Playground

```
const userNames = { firstname: 'Robin', lastname: 'Wieruch' };
const userAge = { age: 28 };
const user = { ...userNames, ...userAge };

console.log(user);
// output: { firstname: 'Robin', lastname: 'Wieruch', age: 28 }
```

After all, it can be used to replace `Object.assign()`.

src/App.js

```
onDismiss(id) {
  const isNotId = item => item.objectID !== id;
  const updatedHits = this.state.result.hits.filter(isNotId);
  this.setState({
    result: { ...this.state.result, hits: updatedHits }
  });
}
```

Now the "Dismiss" button should work again, because the `onDismiss()` method is aware of the complex result object and how to update it after dismissing an item from the list.

Exercises:

- read more about the ES6 Object.assign()[91]
- read more about the ES6 array spread operator[92]
  - the object spread operator is briefly mentioned

---

[91] https://developer.mozilla.org/en/docs/Web/JavaScript/Reference/Global_Objects/Object/assign
[92] https://developer.mozilla.org/en/docs/Web/JavaScript/Reference/Operators/Spread_operator

Conditional Rendering

The conditional rendering is introduced pretty early in React applications. But not in the case of the book, because there wasn't such an use case yet. The conditional rendering happens when you want to make a decision to render either one or another element. Sometimes it means to render an element or nothing. After all, a conditional rendering simplest usage can be expressed by an if-else statement in JSX.

The `result` object in the internal component state is `null` in the beginning. So far, the App component returned no elements when the `result` hasn't arrived from the API. That's already a conditional rendering, because you return earlier from the `render()` lifecycle method for a certain condition. The App component either renders nothing or its elements.

But let's go one step further. It makes more sense to wrap the Table component, which is the only component that depends on the `result`, in an independent conditional rendering. Everything else should be displayed, even though there is no `result` yet. You can simply use a ternary operator in your JSX.

src/App.js

```
class App extends Component {

  ...

  render() {
    const { searchTerm, result } = this.state;
    return (
      <div className="page">
        <div className="interactions">
          <Search
            value={searchTerm}
            onChange={this.onSearchChange}
          >
            Search
          </Search>
        </div>
        { result
          ? <Table
            list={result.hits}
            pattern={searchTerm}
            onDismiss={this.onDismiss}
          />
          : null
        }
```

Getting Real with an API

```
      </div>
    );
  }
}
```

That's your second option to express a conditional rendering. A third option is the logical `&&` operator. In JavaScript a `true && 'Hello World'` always evaluates to 'Hello World'. A `false && 'Hello World'` always evaluates to false.

Code Playground

```
const result = true && 'Hello World';
console.log(result);
// output: Hello World

const result = false && 'Hello World';
console.log(result);
// output: false
```

In React you can make use of that behavior. If the condition is true, the expression after the logical && operator will be the output. If the condition is false, React ignores and skips the expression. It is applicable in the Table conditional rendering case, because it should return a Table or nothing.

src/App.js

```
{ result &&
  <Table
    list={result.hits}
    pattern={searchTerm}
    onDismiss={this.onDismiss}
  />
}
```

These were a few approaches to use conditional rendering in React. You can read about more alternatives in an exhaustive list of examples for conditional rendering approaches[93]. Moreover you will get to know their different use cases and when to apply them.

After all, you should be able to see the fetched data in your application. Everything except the Table is displayed when the data fetching is pending. Once the request resolves the result and stores it into the local state, the Table is displayed because the `render()` method runs again and the condition in the conditional rendering resolves in favor of displaying the Table component.

---

[93]https://www.robinwieruch.de/conditional-rendering-react/

Exercises:

- read more about React conditional rendering[94]
- read more about different ways for conditional renderings[95]

---

[94]https://facebook.github.io/react/docs/conditional-rendering.html
[95]https://www.robinwieruch.de/conditional-rendering-react/

Getting Real with an API

Client- or Server-side Search

When you use the Search component with its input field now, you will filter the happening on the client-side though. Now you are going to use the Hacker News API to search on the server-side. Otherwise you would deal only with the first API response which you got on componentDidMount() with the default search term parameter.

You can define an onSearchSubmit() method in your App component which fetches results from the Hacker News API when executing a search in the Search component. It will be the same fetch as in your componentDidMount() lifecycle method, but this time with a modified search term from the local state and not with the initial default search term.

src/App.js
```
class App extends Component {

  constructor(props) {
    super(props);

    this.state = {
      result: null,
      searchTerm: DEFAULT_QUERY,
    };

    this.setSearchTopStories = this.setSearchTopStories.bind(this);
    this.fetchSearchTopStories = this.fetchSearchTopStories.bind(this);
    this.onSearchChange = this.onSearchChange.bind(this);
    this.onSearchSubmit = this.onSearchSubmit.bind(this);
    this.onDismiss = this.onDismiss.bind(this);
  }

  ...

  onSearchSubmit() {
    const { searchTerm } = this.state;
    this.fetchSearchTopStories(searchTerm);
  }

  ...
}
```

Now the Search component has to add an additional button. The button has to explicitly trigger the search request. Otherwise you would fetch data from the Hacker News API every time when your input field changes. But you want to do it explicitly in a on click handler.

Getting Real with an API

As alternative you could debounce (delay) the onChange() function and spare the button, but it would add more complexity at this time and maybe wouldn't be the desired effect. Let's keep it simple without a debounce for now.

First, pass the onSearchSubmit() method to your Search component.

src/App.js

```
class App extends Component {

  ...

  render() {
    const { searchTerm, result } = this.state;
    return (
      <div className="page">
        <div className="interactions">
          <Search
            value={searchTerm}
            onChange={this.onSearchChange}
            onSubmit={this.onSearchSubmit}
          >
            Search
          </Search>
        </div>
        { result &&
          <Table
            list={result.hits}
            pattern={searchTerm}
            onDismiss={this.onDismiss}
          />
        }
      </div>
    );
  }
}
```

Second, introduce a button in your Search component. The button has the type="submit" and the form uses its onSubmit() attribute to pass the onSubmit() method. You can reuse the children property, but this time it will be used as the content of the button.

src/App.js

```
const Search = ({
  value,
  onChange,
  onSubmit,
  children
}) =>
  <form onSubmit={onSubmit}>
    <input
      type="text"
      value={value}
      onChange={onChange}
    />
    <button type="submit">
      {children}
    </button>
  </form>
```

In the Table, you can remove the filter functionality, because there will be no client-side filter (search) anymore. Don't forget to remove the isSearched() function as well. It will not be used anymore. The result comes directly from the Hacker News API now after you have clicked the "Search" button.

src/App.js

```
class App extends Component {

  ...

  render() {
    const { searchTerm, result } = this.state;
    return (
      <div className="page">
        ...
        { result &&
          <Table
            list={result.hits}
            onDismiss={this.onDismiss}
          />
        }
      </div>
    );
  }
```

Getting Real with an API

```
}

...

const Table = ({ list, onDismiss }) =>
  <div className="table">
    {list.map(item =>
      ...
    )}
  </div>
```

When you try to search now, you will notice that the browser reloads. That's a native browser behavior for a submit callback in a HTML form. In React you will often come across the `preventDefault()` event method to suppress the native browser behavior.

src/App.js

```
onSearchSubmit(event) {
  const { searchTerm } = this.state;
  this.fetchSearchTopStories(searchTerm);
  event.preventDefault();
}
```

Now you should be able to search different Hacker News stories. Perfect, you interact with a real world API. There should be no client-side search anymore.

Exercises:

- read more about synthetic events in React[96]
- experiment with the Hacker News API[97]

---

[96] https://facebook.github.io/react/docs/events.html
[97] https://hn.algolia.com/api

Paginated Fetch

Did you have a closer look at the returned data structure yet? The Hacker News API[98] returns more than a list of hits. Precisely it returns a paginated list. The page property, which is 0 in the first response, can be used to fetch more paginated sublists as result. You only need to pass the next page with the same search term to the API.

Let's extend the composable API constants so that it can deal with paginated data.

src/App.js

```
const DEFAULT_QUERY = 'redux';

const PATH_BASE = 'https://hn.algolia.com/api/v1';
const PATH_SEARCH = '/search';
const PARAM_SEARCH = 'query=';
const PARAM_PAGE = 'page=';
```

Now you can use the new constant to add the page parameter to your API request.

Code Playground

```
const url = `${PATH_BASE}${PATH_SEARCH}?${PARAM_SEARCH}${searchTerm}&${PARAM_PAG\
E}`;

console.log(url);
// output: https://hn.algolia.com/api/v1/search?query=redux&page=
```

The `fetchSearchTopStories()` method will take the page as second argument. If you don't provide the second argument, it will fallback to the 0 page for the initial request. Thus the `componentDidMount()` and `onSearchSubmit()` methods fetch the first page on the first request. Every additional fetch should fetch the next page by providing the second argument.

---

[98] https://hn.algolia.com/api

Getting Real with an API

src/App.js

```
class App extends Component {

  ...

  fetchSearchTopStories(searchTerm, page = 0) {
    fetch(`${PATH_BASE}${PATH_SEARCH}?${PARAM_SEARCH}${searchTerm}&${PARAM_PAGE}\
${page}`)
      .then(response => response.json())
      .then(result => this.setSearchTopStories(result))
      .catch(e => e);
  }

  ...

}
```

Now you can use the current page from the API response in `fetchSearchTopStories()`. You can use this method in a button to fetch more stories on a `onClick` button handler. Let's use the Button to fetch more paginated data from the Hacker News API. You only need to define the `onClick()` handler which takes the current search term and the next page (current page + 1).

src/App.js

```
class App extends Component {

  ...

  render() {
    const { searchTerm, result } = this.state;
    const page = (result && result.page) || 0;
    return (
      <div className="page">
        <div className="interactions">
        ...
          { result &&
            <Table
              list={result.hits}
              onDismiss={this.onDismiss}
            />
          }
        <div className="interactions">
```

implementing page

learn how to connect to an API in Javascript

Getting Real with an API

```
              <Button onClick={() => this.fetchSearchTopStories(searchTerm, page + 1\
)}>
              More
            </Button>
          </div>
        </div>
      );
    }
}
```

In addition, in your render() method you should make sure to default to page 0 when there is no result yet. Remember that the render() method is called before the data is fetched asynchronously in the componentDidMount() lifecycle method.

There is one step missing. You fetch the next page of data, but it will override your previous page of data. It would be ideal to concatenate the old and new list of hits from the local state and new result object. Let's adjust the functionality to add the new data rather than to override it.

src/App.js

```
setSearchTopStories(result) {
  const { hits, page } = result;

  const oldHits = page !== 0
    ? this.state.result.hits
    : [];

  const updatedHits = [
    ...oldHits,
    ...hits
  ];

  this.setState({
    result: { hits: updatedHits, page }
  });
}
```

A couple of things happen in the setSearchTopStories() method now. First, you get the hits and page from the result.

Second, you have to check if there are already old hits. When the page is 0, it is a new search request from componentDidMount() or onSearchSubmit(). The hits are empty. But when you click the "More" button to fetch paginated data the page isn't 0. It is the next page. The old hits are already stored in your state and thus can be used.

Third, you don't want to override the old hits. You can merge old and new hits from the recent API request. The merge of both lists can be done with the JavaScript ES6 array spread operator.

Fourth, you set the merged hits and page in the local component state.

You can make one last adjustment. When you try the "More" button it only fetches a few list items. The API URL can be extended to fetch more list items with each request. Again, you can add more composable path constants.

src/App.js

```
const DEFAULT_QUERY = 'redux';
const DEFAULT_HPP = '100';

const PATH_BASE = 'https://hn.algolia.com/api/v1';
const PATH_SEARCH = '/search';
const PARAM_SEARCH = 'query=';
const PARAM_PAGE = 'page=';
const PARAM_HPP = 'hitsPerPage=';
```

Now you can use the constants to extend the API URL.

src/App.js

```
fetchSearchTopStories(searchTerm, page = 0) {
  fetch(`${PATH_BASE}${PATH_SEARCH}?${PARAM_SEARCH}${searchTerm}&${PARAM_PAGE}${\
page}&${PARAM_HPP}${DEFAULT_HPP}`)
    .then(response => response.json())
    .then(result => this.setSearchTopStories(result))
    .catch(e => e);
}
```

Afterward, the request to the Hacker News API fetches more list items in one request than before. As you can see, a powerful such as the Hacker News API gives you plenty of ways to experiment with real world data. You should make use of it to make your endeavours when learning something new more exciting. That's how I learned about the empowerment that APIs provide[99] when learning a new programming language or library.

Exercises:

- experiment with the Hacker News API parameters[100]

---

[99] https://www.robinwieruch.de/what-is-an-api-javascript/
[100] https://hn.algolia.com/api

Client Cache

Each search submit makes a request to the Hacker News API. You might search for "redux", followed by "react" and eventually "redux" again. In total it makes 3 requests. But you searched for "redux" twice and both times it took a whole asynchronous roundtrip to fetch the data. In a client-sided cache you would store each result. When a request to the API is made, it checks if a result is already there. If it is there, the cache is used. Otherwise an API request is made to fetch the data.

In order to have a client cache for each result, you have to store multiple `results` rather than one `result` in your internal component state. The results object will be a map with the search term as key and the result as value. Each result from the API will be saved by search term (key).

At the moment, your result in the local state looks similar to the following:

Code Playground

```
result: {
  hits: [ ... ],
  page: 2,
}
```

Imagine you have made two API requests. One for the search term "redux" and another one for "react". The results object should look like the following:

Code Playground

```
results: {
  redux: {
    hits: [ ... ],
    page: 2,
  },
  react: {
    hits: [ ... ],
    page: 1,
  },
  ...
}
```

Let's implement a client-side cache with React `setState()`. First, rename the `result` object to `results` in the initial component state. Second, define a temporary `searchKey` which is used to store each `result`.

Getting Real with an API

src/App.js

```
class App extends Component {

  constructor(props) {
    super(props);

    this.state = {
      results: null,
      searchKey: '',
      searchTerm: DEFAULT_QUERY,
    };

    ...

  }

  ...

}
```

The searchKey has to be set before each request is made. It reflects the searchTerm. You might wonder: Why don't we use the searchTerm in the first place? That's a crucial part to understand before continuing with the implementation. The searchTerm is a fluctuant variable, because it gets changed every time you type into the Search input field. However, in the end you will need a non fluctuant variable. It determines the recent submitted search term to the API and can be used to retrieve the correct result from the map of results. It is a pointer to your current result in the cache and thus can be used to display the current result in your render() method.

src/App.js

```
componentDidMount() {
  const { searchTerm } = this.state;
  this.setState({ searchKey: searchTerm });
  this.fetchSearchTopStories(searchTerm);
}

onSearchSubmit(event) {
  const { searchTerm } = this.state;
  this.setState({ searchKey: searchTerm });
  this.fetchSearchTopStories(searchTerm);
  event.preventDefault();
}
```

Now you have to adjust the functionality where the result is stored to the internal component state. It should store each result by searchKey.

src/App.js

```
class App extends Component {

  ...

  setSearchTopStories(result) {
    const { hits, page } = result;
    const { searchKey, results } = this.state;

    const oldHits = results && results[searchKey]
      ? results[searchKey].hits
      : [];

    const updatedHits = [
      ...oldHits,
      ...hits
    ];

    this.setState({
      results: {
        ...results,
        [searchKey]: { hits: updatedHits, page }
      }
    });
  }

  ...

}
```

The searchKey will be used as the key to save the updated hits and page in a results map.

First, you have to retrieve the searchKey from the component state. Remember that the searchKey gets set on componentDidMount() and onSearchSubmit().

Second, the old hits have to get merged with the new hits as before. But this time the old hits get retrieved from the results map with the searchKey as key.

Third, a new result can be set in the results map in the state. Let's examine the results object in setState().

src/App.js

```
results: {
  ...results,
  [searchKey]: { hits: updatedHits, page }
}
```

The bottom part makes sure to store the updated result by searchKey in the results map. The value is an object with a hits and page property. The searchKey is the search term. You already learned the [searchKey]: ... syntax. It is an ES6 computed property name. It helps you to allocate values dynamically in an object.

The upper part needs to spread all other results by searchKey in the state by using the object spread operator. Otherwise you would lose all results that you have stored before.

Now you store all results by search term. That's the first step to enable your cache. In the next step, you can retrieve the result depending on the non fluctuant searchKey from your map of results. That's why you had to introduce the searchKey in the first place as non fluctuant variable. Otherwise the retrieval would be broken when you would use the fluctuant searchTerm to retrieve the current result, because this value might change when you would use the Search component.

src/App.js

```
class App extends Component {

  ...

  render() {
    const {
      searchTerm,
      results,
      searchKey
    } = this.state;

    const page = (
      results &&
      results[searchKey] &&
      results[searchKey].page
    ) || 0;

    const list = (
      results &&
      results[searchKey] &&
      results[searchKey].hits
```

```
    ) || [];

    return (
      <div className="page">
        <div className="interactions">
          ...
        </div>
        <Table
          list={list}
          onDismiss={this.onDismiss}
        />
        <div className="interactions">
          <Button onClick={() => this.fetchSearchTopStories(searchKey, page + 1)\
}>
            More
          </Button>
        </div>
      </div>
    );
  }
}
```

Since you default to an empty list when there is no result by searchKey, you can spare the conditional rendering for the Table component now. Additionally you will need to pass the searchKey rather than the searchTerm to the "More" button. Otherwise your paginated fetch depends on the searchTerm value which is fluctuant. Moreover make sure to keep the fluctuant searchTerm property for the input field in the "Search" component.

The search functionality should work again. It stores all results from the Hacker News API.

Additionally the onDismiss() method needs to get improved. It still deals with the result object. Now it has to deal with multiple results.

src/App.js

```
onDismiss(id) {
  const { searchKey, results } = this.state;
  const { hits, page } = results[searchKey];

  const isNotId = item => item.objectID !== id;
  const updatedHits = hits.filter(isNotId);

  this.setState({
    results: {
```

```
      ...results,
      [searchKey]: { hits: updatedHits, page }
    }
  });
}
```

The "Dismiss" button should work again.

However, nothing stops the application from sending an API request on each search submit. Even though there might be already a result, there is no check that prevents the request. Thus the cache functionality is not complete yet. It caches the results, but it doesn't make use of them. The last step would be to prevent the API request when a result is available in the cache.

src/App.js

```
class App extends Component {

  constructor(props) {

    ...

    this.needsToSearchTopStories = this.needsToSearchTopStories.bind(this);
    this.setSearchTopStories = this.setSearchTopStories.bind(this);
    this.fetchSearchTopStories = this.fetchSearchTopStories.bind(this);
    this.onSearchChange = this.onSearchChange.bind(this);
    this.onSearchSubmit = this.onSearchSubmit.bind(this);
    this.onDismiss = this.onDismiss.bind(this);
  }

  needsToSearchTopStories(searchTerm) {
    return !this.state.results[searchTerm];
  }

  ...

  onSearchSubmit(event) {
    const { searchTerm } = this.state;
    this.setState({ searchKey: searchTerm });

    if (this.needsToSearchTopStories(searchTerm)) {
      this.fetchSearchTopStories(searchTerm);
    }
```

```
    event.preventDefault();
  }

  ...

}
```

Now your client makes a request to the API only once although you search for a search term twice. Even paginated data with several pages gets cached that way, because you always save the last page for each result in the `results` map. Isn't that a powerful approach to introduce caching to your application? The Hacker News API provides you with everything you need to even cache paginated data effectively.

Error Handling

Everything is in place for your interactions with the Hacker News API. You even have introduced an elegant way to cache your results from the API and make use of its paginated list functionality to fetch an endless list of sublists of stories from the API. But there is one piece missing. Unfortunately it is often missed when developing applications nowadays: error handling. It is too easy to implement the happy path without worrying about the errors that can happen along the way.

In this chapter, you will introduce an efficient solution to add error handling for your application in case of an erroneous API request. You have already learned about the necessary building blocks in React to introduce error handling: local state and conditional rendering. Basically, the error is only another state in React. When an error occurs, you will store it in the local state and display it with a conditional rendering in your component. That's it. Let's implement it in the App component, because it's the component that is used to fetch the data from the Hacker News API in the first place. First, you have to introduce the error in the local state. It is initialized as null, but will be set to the error object in case of an error.

src/App.js

```
class App extends Component {
  constructor(props) {
    super(props);

    this.state = {
      results: null,
      searchKey: '',
      searchTerm: DEFAULT_QUERY,
      error: null,
    };

    ...
  }

  ...

}
```

Second, you can use the catch block in your native fetch to store the error object in the local state by using `setState()`. Every time the API request isn't successful, the catch block would be executed.

Getting Real with an API

src/App.js

```
class App extends Component {

  ...

  fetchSearchTopStories(searchTerm, page = 0) {
    fetch(`${PATH_BASE}${PATH_SEARCH}?${PARAM_SEARCH}${searchTerm}&${PARAM_PAGE}\
${page}&${PARAM_HPP}${DEFAULT_HPP}`)
      .then(response => response.json())
      .then(result => this.setSearchTopStories(result))
      .catch(e => this.setState({ error: e }));
  }

  ...

}
```

Third, you can retrieve the error object from your local state in the render() method and display a message in case of an error by using React's conditional rendering.

src/App.js

```
class App extends Component {

  ...

  render() {
    const {
      searchTerm,
      results,
      searchKey,
      error
    } = this.state;

    ...

    if (error) {
      return <p>Something went wrong.</p>;
    }

    return (
      <div className="page">
```

Getting Real with an API

```
      ...
    </div>
  );
 }
}
```

That's it. If you want to test that your error handling is working, you can change the API URL to something else that is non existent.

src/App.js

```
const PATH_BASE = 'https://hn.foo.bar.com/api/v1';
```

Afterward, you should get the error message instead of your application. It is up to you where you want to place the conditional rendering for the error message. In this case, the whole app isn't displayed anymore. That wouldn't be the best user experience. So what about displaying either the Table component or the error message? The remaining application would still be visible in case of an error.

src/App.js

```
class App extends Component {

  ...

  render() {
    const {
      searchTerm,
      results,
      searchKey,
      error
    } = this.state;

    const page = (
      results &&
      results[searchKey] &&
      results[searchKey].page
    ) || 0;

    const list = (
      results &&
      results[searchKey] &&
      results[searchKey].hits
```

Getting Real with an API

```
    ) || [];

    return (
      <div className="page">
        <div className="interactions">
          ...
        </div>
        { error
          ? <div className="interactions">
              <p>Something went wrong.</p>
            </div>
          : <Table
              list={list}
              onDismiss={this.onDismiss}
            />
        }
        ...
      </div>
    );
  }
}
```

In the end, don't forget to revert the URL for the API to the existent one.

src/App.js

```
const PATH_BASE = 'https://hn.algolia.com/api/v1';
```

Your application should still work, but this time with error handling in case the API request fails.

Exercises:

- read more about React's Error Handling for Components[101]

---

[101] https://reactjs.org/blog/2017/07/26/error-handling-in-react-16.html

You have learned to interact with an API in React! Let's recap the last chapters:

- React
    - ES6 class component lifecycle methods for different use cases
    - componentDidMount() for API interactions
    - conditional renderings
    - synthetic events on forms
    - error handling
- ES6
    - template strings to compose strings
    - spread operator for immutable data structures
    - computed property names
- General
    - Hacker News API interaction
    - native fetch browser API
    - client- and server-side search
    - pagination of data
    - client-side caching

Again it makes sense to take a break. Internalize the learnings and apply them on your own. You can experiment with the source code you have written so far.

You can find the source code in the official repository[102].

---
[102] https://github.com/rwieruch/hackernews-client/tree/4.3

Code Organization and Testing

The chapter will focus on important topics to keep your code maintainable in a scaling application. You will learn about code organization to embrace best practices when structuring your folders and files. Another aspect you will learn is testing, which is important to keep your code robust. The whole chapter will take a step back from the practical application and explain a couple of these topics for you.

ES6 Modules: Import and Export

In JavaScript ES6 you can import and export functionalities from modules. These functionalities can be functions, classes, components, constants and others. Basically everything that you can assign to a variable. The modules can be single files or whole folders with one index file as entry point.

In the beginning of the book, after you have bootstrapped your application with *create-react-app*, you already had several import and export statements across your initial files. Now it is the appropriate time to explain these.

The import and export statements help you to share code across multiple files. Before there were already several solutions for this in the JavaScript environment. It was a mess, because you would want to follow one standardized way rather than having several approaches for the same thing. Now it is a native behavior since JavaScript ES6.

Additionally these statements embrace code splitting. You distribute your code across multiple files to keep it reusable and maintainable. The former is true because you can import the piece of code in multiple files. The latter is true because you have one single source where you maintain the piece of code.

Last but not least, it helps you to think about code encapsulation. Not every functionality needs to get exported from a file. Some of these functionalities should only be used in the file where they have been defined. The exports of a file are basically the public API to the file. Only the exported functionalities are available to be reused somewhere else. It follows the best practice of encapsulation.

But let's get practical. How do these import and export statements work? The following examples showcase the statements by sharing one or multiple variables across two files. In the end, the approach can scale to multiple files and could share more than simple variables.

You can export one or multiple variables. It is called a named export.

Code Playground: file1.js

```
const firstname = 'robin';
const lastname = 'wieruch';

export { firstname, lastname };
```

And import them in another file with a relative path to the first file.

Code Playground: file2.js

```
import { firstname, lastname } from './file1.js';

console.log(firstname);
// output: robin
```

You can also import all exported variables from another file as one object.

Code Playground: file2.js

```
import * as person from './file1.js';

console.log(person.firstname);
// output: robin
```

Imports can have an alias. It can happen that you import functionalities from multiple files that have the same named export. That's why you can use an alias.

Code Playground: file2.js

```
import { firstname as foo } from './file1.js';

console.log(foo);
// output: robin
```

Last but not least there exists the `default` statement. It can be used for a few use cases:

- to export and import a single functionality
- to highlight the main functionality of the exported API of a module
- to have a fallback import functionality

Code Playground: file1.js

```
const robin = {
  firstname: 'robin',
  lastname: 'wieruch',
};

export default robin;
```

You can leave out the curly braces for the import to import the default export.

Code Playground: file2.js

```
import developer from './file1.js';

console.log(developer);
// output: { firstname: 'robin', lastname: 'wieruch' }
```

Furthermore, the import name can differ from the exported default name. You can also use it in conjunction with the named export and import statements.

Code Playground: file1.js

```
const firstname = 'robin';
const lastname = 'wieruch';

const person = {
  firstname,
  lastname,
};

export {
  firstname,
  lastname,
};

export default person;
```

Code Playground: file2.js

```
import developer, { firstname, lastname } from './file1.js';

console.log(developer);
// output: { firstname: 'robin', lastname: 'wieruch' }
console.log(firstname, lastname);
// output: robin wieruch
```

In named exports you can spare additional lines and export the variables directly.

Code Playground: file1.js

```
export const firstname = 'robin';
export const lastname = 'wieruch';
```

These are the main functionalities for ES6 modules. They help you to organize your code, to maintain your code and to design reusable module APIs. You can also export and import functionalities to test them. You will do that in one of the following chapters.

Exercises:

- read more about ES6 import[103]
- read more about ES6 export[104]

---

[103] https://developer.mozilla.org/en-US/docs/Web/JavaScript/Reference/Statements/import
[104] https://developer.mozilla.org/en-US/docs/Web/JavaScript/Reference/Statements/export

Code Organization with ES6 Modules

You might wonder: Why didn't we follow the best practices of code splitting for the *src/App.js* file? In the file we already have multiple components which could be defined in their own files/folders (modules). For the sake of learning React, it is practical to keep these things at one place. But once your React application grows, you should consider to split up these components into multiple modules. Only that way your application scales.

In the following, I will propose several module structures you *could* apply. I would recommend to apply them as an exercise at the end of the book. To keep the book itself simple, I will not perform the code splitting and will continue the following chapters with the *src/App.js* file.

One possible module structure could be:

Folder Structure

```
src/
  index.js
  index.css
  App.js
  App.test.js
  App.css
  Button.js
  Button.test.js
  Button.css
  Table.js
  Table.test.js
  Table.css
  Search.js
  Search.test.js
  Search.css
```

It separates the components into their own files, but it doesn't look too promising. You can see a lot of naming duplications and only the file extension differs. Another module structure could be:

Code Organization and Testing

Folder Structure

```
src/
  index.js
  index.css
  App/
    index.js
    test.js
    index.css
  Button/
    index.js
    test.js
    index.css
  Table/
    index.js
    test.js
    index.css
  Search/
    index.js
    test.js
    index.css
```

It looks cleaner than before. The index naming of a file describes it as an entry point file to the folder. It is just a common naming convention, but you can use your own naming as well. In this module structure, a component is defined by its component declaration in the JavaScript file, but also by its style and tests.

Another step could be extracting the constant variables from the App component. These constants were used to compose the Hacker News API URL.

Folder Structure

```
src/
  index.js
  index.css
  constants/
    index.js
  components/
    App/
      index.js
      test.js
      index..css
    Button/
      index.js
```

```
    test.js
    index..css
...
```

Naturally the modules would split up into *src/constants/* and *src/components/*. Now the *src/constants/index.js* file could look like the following:

Code Playground: src/constants/index.js

```
export const DEFAULT_QUERY = 'redux';
export const DEFAULT_HPP = '100';
export const PATH_BASE = 'https://hn.algolia.com/api/v1';
export const PATH_SEARCH = '/search';
export const PARAM_SEARCH = 'query=';
export const PARAM_PAGE = 'page=';
export const PARAM_HPP = 'hitsPerPage=';
```

The *App/index.js* file could import these variables in order to use them.

Code Playground: src/components/App/index.js

```
import {
  DEFAULT_QUERY,
  DEFAULT_HPP,
  PATH_BASE,
  PATH_SEARCH,
  PARAM_SEARCH,
  PARAM_PAGE,
  PARAM_HPP,
} from '../constants/index.js';

...
```

When you use the *index.js* naming convention, you can omit the filename from the relative path.

Code Organization and Testing

Code Playground: src/components/App/index.js

```
import {
  DEFAULT_QUERY,
  DEFAULT_HPP,
  PATH_BASE,
  PATH_SEARCH,
  PARAM_SEARCH,
  PARAM_PAGE,
  PARAM_HPP,
} from '../constants';

...
```

But what's behind the *index.js* file naming? The convention was introduced in the node.js world. The index file is the entry point to a module. It describes the public API to the module. External modules are only allowed to use the *index.js* file to import shared code from the module. Consider the following made up module structure to demonstrate it:

Folder Structure

```
src/
  index.js
  App/
    index.js
  Buttons/
    index.js
    SubmitButton.js
    SaveButton.js
    CancelButton.js
```

The *Buttons/* folder has multiple button components defined in its distinct files. Each file can `export default` the specific component making it available to *Buttons/index.js*. The *Buttons/index.js* file imports all different button representations and exports them as public module API.

/Buttons/index.js

```
.ton from './SubmitButton';
on from './SaveButton';
tton from './CancelButton';

export {
  SubmitButton,
  SaveButton,
  CancelButton,
};
```

Now the *src/App/index.js* can import the buttons from the public module API located in the *index.js* file.

Code Playground: src/App/index.js

```
import {
  SubmitButton,
  SaveButton,
  CancelButton
} from '../Buttons';
```

By going with this constraint, it would be a bad practice to reach into other files than the *index.js* in the module. It would break the rules of encapsulation.

Code Playground: src/App/index.js

```
// bad practice, don't do it
import SubmitButton from '../Buttons/SubmitButton';
```

Now you know how you could refactor your source code in modules with the constraints of encapsulation. As I said, for the sake of keeping the book simple I will not apply these changes. But you should do the refactoring when you finished reading the book.

Exercises:

- refactor your *src/App.js* file into multiple component modules when you finished the book

Snapshot Tests with Jest

The book will not dive deeply into the topic of testing, but it shouldn't be unmentioned. Testing your code in programming is essential and should be seen as mandatory. You want to keep the quality of your code high and an assurance that everything works.

Perhaps you have heard about the testing pyramid. There are end-to-end tests, integration tests and unit tests. If you are not familiar with those, the book gives you a quick and basic overview. A unit test is used to test an isolated and small block of code. It can be a single function that is tested by an unit test. However, sometimes the units work well in isolation yet don't work in combination with other units. They need to be tested as a group as units. That's where integration tests can help out by covering whether units work well together. Last but not least, an end-to-end test is the simulation of a real user scenario. It could be an automated setup in a browser simulating the login flow of an user in a web application. While unit tests are fast and easy to write and to maintain, end-to-end tests are the opposite of this spectrum.

How many tests do I need of each type? You want to have many unit tests to cover your isolated functions. After that, you can have several integration tests to cover that the most important functions work in combination as expected. Last but not least, you might want to have only a few end-to-end tests to simulate critical scenarios in your web application. That's it for the general excursion in the world of testing.

So how do you apply this knowledge in testing your React application? The foundation for testing in React are component tests which can be generalized as unit tests and a part of it as snapshot tests. You will conduct unit tests for your components in the next chapter by using a library called Enzyme. In this chapter, you will focus on another kind of tests: snapshot tests. That's were Jest comes into play.

Jest[105] is a JavaScript testing framework that is used at Facebook. In the React community, it is used for React component tests. Fortunately *create-react-app* already comes with Jest, so you don't need to worry about setting it up.

Let's start to test your first components. Before you can do that, you have to export the components, which you are going to test, from your *src/App.js* file. Afterward you can test them in a different file. You have learned about this in the code organization chapter.

---

[105] https://facebook.github.io/jest/

Code Organization and Testing

src/App.js

```
...

class App extends Component {
  ...
}

...

export default App;

export {
  Button,
  Search,
  Table,
};
```

In your *App.test.js* file, you will find a first test that came with *create-react-app*. It verifies that the App component would render without any errors.

src/App.test.js

```
import React from 'react';
import ReactDOM from 'react-dom';
import App from './App';

it('renders without crashing', () => {
  const div = document.createElement('div');
  ReactDOM.render(<App />, div);
});
```

The "it"-block describes one test case. It comes with a test description and when you test it, it can either succeed or fail. Furthermore, you could wrap it into a "describe"-block that defines your test suit. A test suit could include a bunch of the "it"-blocks for one specific component. You will see those "describe"-blocks later on. Both blocks are used to separated and organize your test cases.

You can run your test cases by using the interactive *create-react-app* test script on the command line. You will get the output for all test cases on your command line interface.

Code Organization and Testing

Command Line

```
npm test
```

Note: If errors show up when you run the single test for the App component for the first time, it could be because of the unsupported fetch method that is used in `fetchSearchTopStories()` which is triggered in `componentDidMount()`. You can make it work by following these two steps:

- On the command line, install the following package: `npm install isomorphic-fetch`
- Include it in your *App.js* file: `import fetch from 'isomorphic-fetch';`

Now Jest enables you to write snapshot tests. These tests make a snapshot of your rendered component and run this snapshot against future snapshots. When a future snapshot changes, you will get notified in the test. You can either accept the snapshot change, because you changed the component implementation on purpose, or deny the change and investigate for the error. It complements unit tests very well, because you only test the diffs of the rendered output. It doesn't add big maintenance costs, because you can simply accept changed snapshots when you changed something on purpose for the rendered output in your component.

Jest stores the snapshots in a folder. Only that way it can validate the diff against a future snapshot. Additionally, the snapshots can be shared across teams by having them in one folder.

Before writing your first snapshot test with Jest, you have to install an utility library.

Command Line

```
npm install --save-dev react-test-renderer
```

Now you can extend the App component test with your first snapshot test. First, import the new functionality from the node package and wrap your previous "it"-block for the App component into a descriptive "describe"-block. In this case, the test suit is only for the App component.

src/App.test.js

```
import React from 'react';
import ReactDOM from 'react-dom';
import renderer from 'react-test-renderer';
import App from './App';

describe('App', () => {

  it('renders without crashing', () => {
    const div = document.createElement('div');
    ReactDOM.render(<App />, div);
```

Code Organization and Testing

```
  });

});
```

Now you can implement your first snapshot test by using a "test"-block.

src/App.test.js

```
import React from 'react';
import ReactDOM from 'react-dom';
import renderer from 'react-test-renderer';
import App from './App';

describe('App', () => {

  it('renders without crashing', () => {
    const div = document.createElement('div');
    ReactDOM.render(<App />, div);
  });

  test('has a valid snapshot', () => {
    const component = renderer.create(
      <App />
    );
    let tree = component.toJSON();
    expect(tree).toMatchSnapshot();
  });

});
```

Run your tests again and see how the tests either succeed or fail. They should succeed. Once you change the output of the render block in your App component, the snapshot test should fail. Then you can decide to update the snapshot or investigate in your App component.

Basically the `renderer.create()` function creates a snapshot of your App component. It renders it virtually and stores the DOM into a snapshot. Afterward, the snapshot is expected to match the previous snapshot from when you ran your snapshot tests the last time. This way, you can assure that your DOM stays the same and doesn't change anything by accident.

Let's add more tests for our independent components. First, the Search component:

Code Organization and Testing   129

src/App.test.js

```
import React from 'react';
import ReactDOM from 'react-dom';
import renderer from 'react-test-renderer';
import App, { Search } from './App';

...

describe('Search', () => {

  it('renders without crashing', () => {
    const div = document.createElement('div');
    ReactDOM.render(<Search>Search</Search>, div);
  });

  test('has a valid snapshot', () => {
    const component = renderer.create(
      <Search>Search</Search>
    );
    let tree = component.toJSON();
    expect(tree).toMatchSnapshot();
  });

});
```

The Search component has two tests similar to the App component. The first test simply renders the Search component to the DOM and verifies that there is no error during the rendering process. If there would be an error, the test would break even though there isn't any assertion (e.g. expect, match, equal) in the test block. The second snapshot test is used to store a snapshot of the rendered component and to run it against a previous snapshot. It fails when the snapshot has changed.

Second, you can test the Button component whereas the same test rules as in the Search component apply.

Code Organization and Testing

src/App.test.js

```
...
import App, { Search, Button } from './App';

...

describe('Button', () => {

  it('renders without crashing', () => {
    const div = document.createElement('div');
    ReactDOM.render(<Button>Give Me More</Button>, div);
  });

  test('has a valid snapshot', () => {
    const component = renderer.create(
      <Button>Give Me More</Button>
    );
    let tree = component.toJSON();
    expect(tree).toMatchSnapshot();
  });

});
```

Last but not least, the Table component that you can pass a bunch of initial props to render it with a sample list.

src/App.test.js

```
...
import App, { Search, Button, Table } from './App';

...

describe('Table', () => {

  const props = {
    list: [
      { title: '1', author: '1', num_comments: 1, points: 2, objectID: 'y' },
      { title: '2', author: '2', num_comments: 1, points: 2, objectID: 'z' },
    ],
  };
```

```
  it('renders without crashing', () => {
    const div = document.createElement('div');
    ReactDOM.render(<Table { ...props } />, div);
  });

  test('has a valid snapshot', () => {
    const component = renderer.create(
      <Table { ...props } />
    );
    let tree = component.toJSON();
    expect(tree).toMatchSnapshot();
  });

});
```

Snapshot tests usually stay pretty basic. You only want to cover that the component doesn't change its output. Once it changes the output, you have to decide if you accept the changes. Otherwise you have to fix the component when the output is not the desired output.

Exercises:

- see how a snapshot test fails once you change your component's return value in the render() method
    - either accept or deny the snapshot change
- keep your snapshots tests up to date when the implementation of components change in next chapters
- read more about Jest in React[106]

---

[106] https://facebook.github.io/jest/docs/tutorial-react.html

Unit Tests with Enzyme

Enzyme[107] is a testing utility by Airbnb to assert, manipulate and traverse your React components. You can use it to conduct unit tests to complement your snapshot tests in React.

Let's see how you can use enzyme. First you have to install it since it doesn't come by default with *create-react-app*. It comes also with an extension to use it in React.

Command Line

```
npm install --save-dev enzyme react-addons-test-utils enzyme-adapter-react-16
```

Second, you need to include it in your test setup and initialize its Adapter for using it in React.

src/App.test.js

```
import React from 'react';
import ReactDOM from 'react-dom';
import renderer from 'react-test-renderer';
import Enzyme from 'enzyme';
import Adapter from 'enzyme-adapter-react-16';
import App, { Search, Button, Table } from './App';

Enzyme.configure({ adapter: new Adapter() });
```

Now you can write your first unit test in the Table "describe"-block. You will use `shallow()` to render your component and assert that the Table has two items, because you pass it two list items. The assertion simply checks if the element has two elements with the class `table-row`.

src/App.test.js

```
import React from 'react';
import ReactDOM from 'react-dom';
import renderer from 'react-test-renderer';
import Enzyme, { shallow } from 'enzyme';
import Adapter from 'enzyme-adapter-react-16';
import App, { Search, Button, Table } from './App';

...

describe('Table', () => {
```

---

[107] https://github.com/airbnb/enzyme

```
  const props = {
    list: [
      { title: '1', author: '1', num_comments: 1, points: 2, objectID: 'y' },
      { title: '2', author: '2', num_comments: 1, points: 2, objectID: 'z' },
    ],
  };

  ...

  it('shows two items in list', () => {
    const element = shallow(
      <Table { ...props } />
    );

    expect(element.find('.table-row').length).toBe(2);
  });

});
```

Shallow renders the component without its child components. That way, you can make the test very dedicated to one component.

Enzyme has overall three rendering mechanisms in its API. You already know shallow(), but there also exist mount() and render(). Both instantiate instances of the parent component and all child components. Additionally mount() gives you access to the component lifecycle methods. But when to use which render mechanism? Here some rules of thumb:

- Always begin with a shallow test
- If componentDidMount() or componentDidUpdate() should be tested, use mount()
- If you want to test component lifecycle and children behavior, use mount()
- If you want to test a component's children rendering with less overhead than mount() and you are not interested in lifecycle methods, use render()

You could continue to unit test your components. But make sure to keep the tests simple and maintainable. Otherwise you will have to refactor them once you change your components. That's why Facebook introduced snapshot tests with Jest in the first place.

Exercises:

- write a unit test with Enzyme for your Button component
- keep your unit tests up to date during the following chapters
- read more about enzyme and its rendering API[108]

---

[108]https://github.com/airbnb/enzyme

Component Interface with PropTypes

You may know TypeScript[109] or Flow[110] to introduce a type interface to JavaScript. A typed language is less error prone, because the code gets validated based on its program text. Editors and other utilities can catch these errors before the program runs. It makes your program more robust.

In the book, you will not introduce Flow or TypeScript, but another neat way to check your types in components. React comes with a built-in type checker to prevent bugs. You can use PropTypes to describe your component interface. All the props that get passed from a parent component to a child component get validated based on the PropTypes interface assigned to the child component.

The chapter will show you how you can make all your components type safe with PropTypes. I will omit the changes for the following chapters, because they add unnecessary code refactorings. But you should keep and update them along the way to keep your components interface type safe.

First, you have to install a separate package for React.

Command Line

```
npm install prop-types
```

Now, you can import the PropTypes.

src/App.js

```
import PropTypes from 'prop-types';
```

Let's start to assign a props interface to the components:

src/App.js

```
const Button = ({ onClick, className = '', children }) =>
  <button
    onClick={onClick}
    className={className}
    type="button"
  >
    {children}
  </button>

Button.propTypes = {
  onClick: PropTypes.func,
```

---

[109] https://www.typescriptlang.org/
[110] https://flowtype.org/

```
  className: PropTypes.string,
  children: PropTypes.node,
};
```

Basically that's it. You take every argument from the function signature and assign a PropType to it. The basic PropTypes for primitives and complex objects are:

- PropTypes.array
- PropTypes.bool
- PropTypes.func
- PropTypes.number
- PropTypes.object
- PropTypes.string

Additionally you have two more PropTypes to define a renderable fragment (node), e.g. a string, and a React element:

- PropTypes.node
- PropTypes.element

You already used the `node` PropType for the Button component. Overall there are more PropType definitions that you can read up in the official React documentation.

At the moment all of the defined PropTypes for the Button are optional. The parameters can be null or undefined. But for several props you want to enforce that they are defined. You can make it a requirement that these props are passed to the component.

src/App.js

```
Button.propTypes = {
  onClick: PropTypes.func.isRequired,
  className: PropTypes.string,
  children: PropTypes.node.isRequired,
};
```

The `className` is not required, because it can default to an empty string. Next you will define a PropType interface for the Table component:

Code Organization and Testing 136

src/App.js

```
Table.propTypes = {
  list: PropTypes.array.isRequired,
  onDismiss: PropTypes.func.isRequired,
};
```

You can define the content of an array PropType more explicit:

src/App.js

```
Table.propTypes = {
  list: PropTypes.arrayOf(
    PropTypes.shape({
      objectID: PropTypes.string.isRequired,
      author: PropTypes.string,
      url: PropTypes.string,
      num_comments: PropTypes.number,
      points: PropTypes.number,
    })
  ).isRequired,
  onDismiss: PropTypes.func.isRequired,
};
```

Only the `objectID` is required, because you know that some of your code depends on it. The other properties are only displayed, thus they are not necessarily required. Moreover you cannot be sure that the Hacker News API has always a defined property for each object in the array.

That's it for PropTypes. But there is one more aspect. You can define default props in your component. Let's take again the Button component. The `className` property has an ES6 default parameter in the component signature.

src/App.js

```
const Button = ({
  onClick,
  className = '',
  children
}) =>
  ...
```

You could replace it with the internal React default prop:

Code Organization and Testing

src/App.js

```
const Button = ({
  onClick,
  className,
  children
}) =>
  <button
    onClick={onClick}
    className={className}
    type="button"
  >
    {children}
  </button>

Button.defaultProps = {
  className: '',
};
```

Same as the ES6 default parameter, the default prop ensures that the property is set to a default value when the parent component didn't specify it. The PropType type check happens after the default prop is evaluated.

If you run your tests again, you might see PropType errors for your components on your command line. It can happen because you didn't define all props for your components in the tests that are defined as required in your PropType definition. The tests themselves all pass correctly though. You can pass all required props to avoid these errors.

Exercises:

- define the PropType interface for the Search component
- add and update the PropType interfaces when you add and update components in the next chapters
- read more about React PropTypes[111]

---

[111]https://facebook.github.io/react/docs/typechecking-with-proptypes.html

You have learned how to organize your code and how to test it! Let's recap the last chapters:

- React
    - PropTypes let you define type checks for components
    - Jest allows you to write snapshot tests for your components
    - Enzyme allows you to write unit tests for your components
- ES6
    - import and export statements help you to organize your code
- General
    - code organization allows you to scale your application with best practices

You can find the source code in the official repository[112].

---
[112] https://github.com/rwieruch/hackernews-client/tree/4.4

Advanced React Components

The chapter will focus on the implementation of advanced React components. You will learn about higher order components and how to implement them. In addition you will dive into more advanced topics in React and implement complex interactions with it.

Ref a DOM Element

Sometimes you need to interact with your DOM nodes in React. The `ref` attribute gives you access to a node in your elements. Usually that is an anti pattern in React, because you should use its declarative way of doing things and its unidirectional data flow. You have learned about it when you have introduced your first search input field. But there are certain cases where you need access to the DOM node. The official documentation mentions three use cases:

- to use the DOM API (focus, media playback etc.)
- to invoke imperative DOM node animations
- to integrate with third-party library that needs the DOM node (e.g. D3.js[113])

Let's do it by example with the Search component. When the application renders the first time, the input field should be focused. That's one use case where you would need access to the DOM API. This chapter will show you how it works, but since it is not very useful for the application itself, we will omit the changes after the chapter. You can keep it for your own application though.

In general, you can use the `ref` attribute in both functional stateless components and ES6 class components. In the example of the focus use case, you will need a lifecycle method. That's why the approach is first showcased by using the `ref` attribute with an ES6 class component.

The initial step is to refactor the functional stateless component to an ES6 class component.

src/App.js

```
class Search extends Component {
  render() {
    const {
      value,
      onChange,
      onSubmit,
      children
    } = this.props;

    return (
      <form onSubmit={onSubmit}>
        <input
          type="text"
          value={value}
          onChange={onChange}
        />
        <button type="submit">
```

---

[113]https://d3js.org/

```
        {children}
      </button>
    </form>
  );
  }
}
```

The `this` object of an ES6 class component helps us to reference the DOM node with the `ref` attribute.

src/App.js

```
class Search extends Component {
  render() {
    const {
      value,
      onChange,
      onSubmit,
      children
    } = this.props;

    return (
      <form onSubmit={onSubmit}>
        <input
          type="text"
          value={value}
          onChange={onChange}
          ref={(node) => { this.input = node; }}
        />
        <button type="submit">
          {children}
        </button>
      </form>
    );
  }
}
```

Now you can focus the input field when the component mounted by using the `this` object, the appropriate lifecycle method, and the DOM API.

src/App.js

```
class Search extends Component {
  componentDidMount() {
    this.input.focus();
  }

  render() {
    const {
      value,
      onChange,
      onSubmit,
      children
    } = this.props;

    return (
      <form onSubmit={onSubmit}>
        <input
          type="text"
          value={value}
          onChange={onChange}
          ref={(node) => { this.input = node; }}
        />
        <button type="submit">
          {children}
        </button>
      </form>
    );
  }
}
```

The input field should be focused when the application renders. That's it basically for using the ref attribute.

But how would you get access to the ref in a functional stateless component without the this object? The following functional stateless component demonstrates it.

Advanced React Components

src/App.js

```
const Search = ({
  value,
  onChange,
  onSubmit,
  children
}) => {
  let input;
  return (
    <form onSubmit={onSubmit}>
      <input
        type="text"
        value={value}
        onChange={onChange}
        ref={(node) => input = node}
      />
      <button type="submit">
        {children}
      </button>
    </form>
  );
}
```

Now you would be able to access the input DOM element. In the example of the focus use case it wouldn't help you, because you have no lifecycle method in a functional stateless component to trigger the focus. But in the future you might come across other use cases where it can make sense to use a functional stateless component with the `ref` attribute.

Exercises

- read more about the ref attribute in general in React[114]
- read more about the usage of the ref attribute in React[115]

---

[114] https://facebook.github.io/react/docs/refs-and-the-dom.html
[115] https://www.robinwieruch.de/react-ref-attribute-dom-node/

Loading ...

Now let's get back to the application. You might want to show a loading indicator when you submit a search request to the Hacker News API. The request is asynchronous and you should show your user some feedback that something is about to happen. Let's define a reusable Loading component in your *src/App.js* file.

src/App.js

```
const Loading = () =>
  <div>Loading ...</div>
```

Now you will need a property to store the loading state. Based on the loading state you can decide to show the Loading component later on.

src/App.js

```
class App extends Component {

  constructor(props) {
    super(props);

    this.state = {
      results: null,
      searchKey: '',
      searchTerm: DEFAULT_QUERY,
      error: null,
      isLoading: false,
    };

    ...
  }

  ...

}
```

The initial value of that `isLoading` property is false. You don't load anything before the App component is mounted.

When you make the request, you set a loading state to true. Eventually the request will succeed and you can set the loading state to false.

src/App.js

```
class App extends Component {

  ...

  setSearchTopStories(result) {
    ...

    this.setState({
      results: {
        ...results,
        [searchKey]: { hits: updatedHits, page }
      },
      isLoading: false
    });
  }

  fetchSearchTopStories(searchTerm, page = 0) {
    this.setState({ isLoading: true });

    fetch(`${PATH_BASE}${PATH_SEARCH}?${PARAM_SEARCH}${searchTerm}&${PARAM_PAGE}\
${page}&${PARAM_HPP}${DEFAULT_HPP}`)
      .then(response => response.json())
      .then(result => this.setSearchTopStories(result))
      .catch(e => this.setState({ error: e }));
  }

  ...

}
```

In the last step, you will use the Loading component in your App. A conditional rendering based on the loading state will decide whether you show a Loading component or the Button component. The latter one is your button to fetch more data.

src/App.js

```
class App extends Component {

  ...

  render() {
    const {
      searchTerm,
      results,
      searchKey,
      error,
      isLoading
    } = this.state;

    ...

    return (
      <div className="page">
        ...
        <div className="interactions">
          { isLoading
            ? <Loading />
            : <Button
              onClick={() => this.fetchSearchTopStories(searchKey, page + 1)}>
              More
            </Button>
          }
        </div>
      </div>
    );
  }
}
```

Initially the Loading component will show up when you start your application, because you make a request on componentDidMount(). There is no Table component, because the list is empty. When the response returns from the Hacker News API, the result is shown, the loading state is set to false and the Loading component disappears. Instead, the "More" button to fetch more data appears. Once you fetch more data, the button will disappear again and the Loading component will show up.

Exercises:

- use a library such as Font Awesome[116] to show a loading icon instead of the "Loading ..." text

---

[116]http://fontawesome.io/

Higher Order Components

Higher order components (HOC) are an advanced concept in React. HOCs are an equivalent to higher order functions. They take any input - most of the time a component, but also optional arguments - and return a component as output. The returned component is an enhanced version of the input component and can be used in your JSX.

HOCs are used for different use cases. They can prepare properties, manage state or alter the representation of a component. One use case could be to use a HOC as a helper for a conditional rendering. Imagine you have a List component that renders a list of items or nothing, because the list is empty or null. The HOC could shield away that the list would render nothing when there is no list. On the other hand, the plain List component doesn't need to bother anymore about an non existent list. It only cares about rendering the list.

Let's do a simple HOC which takes a component as input and returns a component. You can place it in your *src/App.js* file.

src/App.js

```
function withFoo(Component) {
  return function(props) {
    return <Component { ...props } />;
  }
}
```

One neat convention is to prefix the naming of a HOC with `with`. Since you are using JavaScript ES6, you can express the HOC more concisely with an ES6 arrow function.

src/App.js

```
const withFoo = (Component) => (props) =>
  <Component { ...props } />
```

In the example, the input component would stay the same as the output component. Nothing happens. It renders the same component instance and passes all of the props to the output component. But that's useless. Let's enhance the output component. The output component should show the Loading component, when the loading state is true, otherwise it should show the input component. A conditional rendering is a great use case for a HOC.

Advanced React Components

src/App.js

```
const withLoading = (Component) => (props) =>
  props.isLoading
    ? <Loading />
    : <Component { ...props } />
```

Based on the loading property you can apply a conditional rendering. The function will return the Loading component or the input component.

In general it can be very efficient to spread an object, like the props object in the previous example, as input for a component. See the difference in the following code snippet.

Code Playground

```
// before you would have to destructure the props before passing them
const { foo, bar } = props;
<SomeComponent foo={foo} bar={bar} />

// but you can use the object spread operator to pass all object properties
<SomeComponent { ...props } />
```

There is one little thing that you should avoid. You pass all the props including the isLoading property, by spreading the object, into the input component. However, the input component may not care about the isLoading property. You can use the ES6 rest destructuring to avoid it.

src/App.js

```
const withLoading = (Component) => ({ isLoading, ...rest }) =>
  isLoading
    ? <Loading />
    : <Component { ...rest } />
```

It takes one property out of the object, but keeps the remaining object. It works with multiple properties as well. You might have already read about it in the destructuring assignment[117].

Now you can use the HOC in your JSX. An use case in the application could be to show either the "More" button or the Loading component. The Loading component is already encapsulated in the HOC, but an input component is missing. In the use case of showing a Button component or a Loading component, the Button is the input component of the HOC. The enhanced output component is a ButtonWithLoading component.

---

[117]https://developer.mozilla.org/en-US/docs/Web/JavaScript/Reference/Operators/Destructuring_assignment

Advanced React Components

src/App.js

```
const Button = ({ onClick, className = '', children }) =>
  <button
    onClick={onClick}
    className={className}
    type="button"
  >
    {children}
  </button>

const Loading = () =>
  <div>Loading ...</div>

const withLoading = (Component) => ({ isLoading, ...rest }) =>
  isLoading
    ? <Loading />
    : <Component { ...rest } />

const ButtonWithLoading = withLoading(Button);
```

Everything is defined now. As a last step, you have to use the ButtonWithLoading component, which receives the loading state as an additional property. While the HOC consumes the loading property, all other props get passed to the Button component.

src/App.js

```
class App extends Component {

  ...

  render() {
    ...
    return (
      <div className="page">
        ...
        <div className="interactions">
          <ButtonWithLoading
            isLoading={isLoading}
            onClick={() => this.fetchSearchTopStories(searchKey, page + 1)}>
            More
          </ButtonWithLoading>
        </div>
```

Advanced React Components

```
      </div>
    );
  }
}
```

When you run your tests again, you will notice that your snapshot test for the App component fails. The diff might look like the following on the command line:

Command Line

```
-    <button
-      className=""
-      onClick={[Function]}
-      type="button"
-    >
-      More
-    </button>
+    <div>
+      Loading ...
+    </div>
```

You can either fix the component now, when you think there is something wrong about it, or can accept the new snapshot of it. Because you introduced the Loading component in this chapter, you can accept the altered snapshot test on the command line in the interactive test.

Higher order components are an advanced technique in React. They have multiple purposes like improved reusability of components, greater abstraction, composability of components and manipulations of props, state and view. Don't worry if you don't understand them immediately. It takes time to get used to them.

I encourage you to read the gentle introduction to higher order components[118]. It gives you another approach to learn them, shows you an elegant way to use them a functional programming way and solves specifically the problem of conditional rendering with higher order components.

Exercises:

- read a gentle introduction to higher order components[119]
- experiment with the HOC you have created
- think about a use case where another HOC would make sense
    - implement the HOC, if there is a use case

---

[118] https://www.robinwieruch.de/gentle-introduction-higher-order-components/
[119] https://www.robinwieruch.de/gentle-introduction-higher-order-components/

Advanced Sorting

You have already implemented a client- and server-side search interaction. Since you have a Table component, it would make sense to enhance the Table with advanced interactions. What about introducing a sort functionality for each column by using the column headers of the Table?

It would be possible to write your own sort function, but personally I prefer to use a utility library for such cases. Lodash[120] is one of these utility libraries, but you can use whatever library suits you. Let's install Lodash and use it for the sort functionality.

Command Line

```
npm install lodash
```

Now you can import the sort functionality of Lodash in your *src/App.js* file.

src/App.js

```
import React, { Component } from 'react';
import fetch from 'isomorphic-fetch';
import { sortBy } from 'lodash';
import './App.css';
```

You have several columns in your Table. There are title, author, comments and points columns. You can define sort functions whereas each function takes a list and returns a list of items sorted by a specific property. Additionally, you will need one default sort function which doesn't sort but only returns the unsorted list. That will be your initial state.

src/App.js

```
...

const SORTS = {
  NONE: list => list,
  TITLE: list => sortBy(list, 'title'),
  AUTHOR: list => sortBy(list, 'author'),
  COMMENTS: list => sortBy(list, 'num_comments').reverse(),
  POINTS: list => sortBy(list, 'points').reverse(),
};

class App extends Component {
  ...
}
...
```

---

[120] https://lodash.com/

Advanced React Components

You can see that two of the sort functions return a reversed list. That's because you want to see the items with the highest comments and points rather than to see the items with the lowest counts when you sort the list for the first time.

The SORTS object allows you to reference any sort function now.

Again your App component is responsible for storing the state of the sort. The initial state will be the initial default sort function, which doesn't sort at all and returns the input list as output.

src/App.js

```
this.state = {
  results: null,
  searchKey: '',
  searchTerm: DEFAULT_QUERY,
  error: null,
  isLoading: false,
  sortKey: 'NONE',
};
```

Once you choose a different sortKey, let's say the AUTHOR key, you will sort the list with the appropriate sort function from the SORTS object.

Now you can define a new class method in your App component that simply sets a sortKey to your local component state. Afterward, the sortKey can be used to retrieve the sorting function to apply it on your list.

src/App.js

```
class App extends Component {

  constructor(props) {

    ...

    this.needsToSearchTopStories = this.needsToSearchTopStories.bind(this);
    this.setSearchTopStories = this.setSearchTopStories.bind(this);
    this.fetchSearchTopStories = this.fetchSearchTopStories.bind(this);
    this.onSearchSubmit = this.onSearchSubmit.bind(this);
    this.onSearchChange = this.onSearchChange.bind(this);
    this.onDismiss = this.onDismiss.bind(this);
    this.onSort = this.onSort.bind(this);
  }

  onSort(sortKey) {
```

```
    this.setState({ sortKey });
  }

  ...

}
```

The next step is to pass the method and sortKey to your Table component.

src/App.js

```
class App extends Component {

  ...

  render() {
    const {
      searchTerm,
      results,
      searchKey,
      error,
      isLoading,
      sortKey
    } = this.state;

    ...

    return (
      <div className="page">
        ...
        <Table
          list={list}
          sortKey={sortKey}
          onSort={this.onSort}
          onDismiss={this.onDismiss}
        />
        ...
      </div>
    );
  }
}
```

Advanced React Components

The Table component is responsible for sorting the list. It takes one of the SORT functions by sortKey and passes the list as input. Afterward it keeps mapping over the sorted list.

src/App.js

```
const Table = ({
  list,
  sortKey,
  onSort,
  onDismiss
}) =>
  <div className="table">
    {SORTS[sortKey](list).map(item =>
      <div key={item.objectID} className="table-row">
        ...
      </div>
    )}
  </div>
```

In theory the list would get sorted by one of the functions. But the default sort is set to NONE, so nothing is sorted yet. So far, no one executes the onSort() method to change the sortKey. Let's extend the Table with a row of column headers that use Sort components in columns to sort each column.

src/App.js

```
const Table = ({
  list,
  sortKey,
  onSort,
  onDismiss
}) =>
  <div className="table">
    <div className="table-header">
      <span style={{ width: '40%' }}>
        <Sort
          sortKey={'TITLE'}
          onSort={onSort}
        >
          Title
        </Sort>
      </span>
      <span style={{ width: '30%' }}>
```

```
        <Sort
          sortKey={'AUTHOR'}
          onSort={onSort}
        >
          Author
        </Sort>
      </span>
      <span style={{ width: '10%' }}>
        <Sort
          sortKey={'COMMENTS'}
          onSort={onSort}
        >
          Comments
        </Sort>
      </span>
      <span style={{ width: '10%' }}>
        <Sort
          sortKey={'POINTS'}
          onSort={onSort}
        >
          Points
        </Sort>
      </span>
      <span style={{ width: '10%' }}>
        Archive
      </span>
    </div>
    {SORTS[sortKey](list).map(item =>
      ...
    )}
  </div>
```

Each Sort component gets a specific `sortKey` and the general `onSort()` function. Internally it calls the method with the `sortKey` to set the specific key.

src/App.js

```
const Sort = ({ sortKey, onSort, children }) =>
  <Button onClick={() => onSort(sortKey)}>
    {children}
  </Button>
```

Advanced React Components

As you can see, the Sort component reuses your common Button component. On a button click each individual passed sortKey will get set by the onSort() method. Now you should be able to sort the list when you click on the column headers.

There is one minor improvement for an improved look. So far, the button in a column header looks a bit silly. Let's give the button in the Sort component a proper className.

src/App.js

```
const Sort = ({ sortKey, onSort, children }) =>
  <Button
    onClick={() => onSort(sortKey)}
    className="button-inline"
  >
    {children}
  </Button>
```

It should look nice now. The next goal would be to implement a reverse sort as well. The list should get reverse sorted once you click a Sort component twice. First, you need to define the reverse state with a boolean. The sort can be either reversed or non reversed.

src/App.js

```
this.state = {
  results: null,
  searchKey: '',
  searchTerm: DEFAULT_QUERY,
  error: null,
  isLoading: false,
  sortKey: 'NONE',
  isSortReverse: false,
};
```

Now in your sort method, you can evaluate if the list is reverse sorted. It is reverse if the sortKey in the state is the same as the incoming sortKey and the reverse state is not already set to true.

Advanced React Components

src/App.js

```
onSort(sortKey) {
  const isSortReverse = this.state.sortKey === sortKey && !this.state.isSortReve\
rse;
  this.setState({ sortKey, isSortReverse });
}
```

Again you can pass the reverse prop to your Table component.

src/App.js

```
class App extends Component {

  ...

  render() {
    const {
      searchTerm,
      results,
      searchKey,
      error,
      isLoading,
      sortKey,
      isSortReverse
    } = this.state;

    ...

    return (
      <div className="page">
        ...
        <Table
          list={list}
          sortKey={sortKey}
          isSortReverse={isSortReverse}
          onSort={this.onSort}
          onDismiss={this.onDismiss}
        />
        ...
      </div>
    );
  }
}
```

Advanced React Components

The Table has to have an arrow function block body to compute the data now.

src/App.js

```
const Table = ({
  list,
  sortKey,
  isSortReverse,
  onSort,
  onDismiss
}) => {
  const sortedList = SORTS[sortKey](list);
  const reverseSortedList = isSortReverse
    ? sortedList.reverse()
    : sortedList;

  return(
    <div className="table">
      <div className="table-header">
        ...
      </div>
      {reverseSortedList.map(item =>
        ...
      )}
    </div>
  );
}
```

The reverse sort should work now.

Last but not least, you have to deal with one open question for the sake of an improved user experience. Can a user distinguish which column is actively sorted? So far, it is not possible. Let's give the user a visual feedback.

Each Sort component gets its specific sortKey already. It could be used to identify the activated sort. You can pass the sortKey from the internal component state as active sort key to your Sort component.

src/App.js

```
const Table = ({
  list,
  sortKey,
  isSortReverse,
  onSort,
  onDismiss
}) => {
  const sortedList = SORTS[sortKey](list);
  const reverseSortedList = isSortReverse
    ? sortedList.reverse()
    : sortedList;

  return(
    <div className="table">
      <div className="table-header">
        <span style={{ width: '40%' }}>
          <Sort
            sortKey={'TITLE'}
            onSort={onSort}
            activeSortKey={sortKey}
          >
            Title
          </Sort>
        </span>
        <span style={{ width: '30%' }}>
          <Sort
            sortKey={'AUTHOR'}
            onSort={onSort}
            activeSortKey={sortKey}
          >
            Author
          </Sort>
        </span>
        <span style={{ width: '10%' }}>
          <Sort
            sortKey={'COMMENTS'}
            onSort={onSort}
            activeSortKey={sortKey}
          >
            Comments
          </Sort>
```

Advanced React Components

```
          </span>
          <span style={{ width: '10%' }}>
            <Sort
              sortKey={'POINTS'}
              onSort={onSort}
              activeSortKey={sortKey}
            >
              Points
            </Sort>
          </span>
          <span style={{ width: '10%' }}>
            Archive
          </span>
        </div>
        {reverseSortedList.map(item =>
            ...
        )}
      </div>
    );
}
```

Now in your Sort component, you know based on the sortKey and activeSortKey whether the sort is active. Give your Sort component an extra className attribute, in case it is sorted, to give the user a visual feedback.

src/App.js

```
const Sort = ({
  sortKey,
  activeSortKey,
  onSort,
  children
}) => {
  const sortClass = ['button-inline'];

  if (sortKey === activeSortKey) {
    sortClass.push('button-active');
  }

  return (
    <Button
      onClick={() => onSort(sortKey)}
      className={sortClass.join(' ')}
```

```
      >
        {children}
      </Button>
  );
}
```

The way to define the sortClass is a bit clumsy, isn't it? There is a neat little library to get rid of this. First you have to install it.

Command Line

```
npm install classnames
```

And second you have to import it on top of your *src/App.js* file.

src/App.js

```
import React, { Component } from 'react';
import fetch from 'isomorphic-fetch';
import { sortBy } from 'lodash';
import classNames from 'classnames';
import './App.css';
```

Now you can use it to define your component className with conditional classes.

src/App.js

```
const Sort = ({
  sortKey,
  activeSortKey,
  onSort,
  children
}) => {
  const sortClass = classNames(
    'button-inline',
    { 'button-active': sortKey === activeSortKey }
  );

  return (
    <Button
      onClick={() => onSort(sortKey)}
      className={sortClass}
    >
```

Advanced React Components

```
      {children}
    </Button>
  );
}
```

Again, when you run your tests, you should see failing snapshot tests but also failing unit tests for the Table component. Since you changed again your component representations, you can accept the snapshot tests. But you have to fix the unit test. In your *src/App.test.js* file, you need to provide a sortKey and the isSortReverse boolean for the Table component.

src/App.test.js

```
...

describe('Table', () => {

  const props = {
    list: [
      { title: '1', author: '1', num_comments: 1, points: 2, objectID: 'y' },
      { title: '2', author: '2', num_comments: 1, points: 2, objectID: 'z' },
    ],
    sortKey: 'TITLE',
    isSortReverse: false,
  };

  ...

});
```

Once again you might need to accept the failing snapshot tests for your Table component, because you provided extended props for the Table component.

Finally your advanced sort interaction is complete now.

Exercises:

- use a library like Font Awesome[121] to indicate the (reverse) sort
    - it could be an arrow up or arrow down icon next to each Sort header
- read more about the classnames library[122]

---

[121] http://fontawesome.io/
[122] https://github.com/JedWatson/classnames

Advanced React Components

You have learned advanced component techniques in React! Let's recap the last chapters:

- React
    - the ref attribute to reference DOM nodes
    - higher order components are a common way to build advanced components
    - implementation of advanced interactions in React
    - conditional classNames with a neat helper library
- ES6
    - rest destructuring to split up objects and arrays

You can find the source code in the official repository[123].

---

[123]https://github.com/rwieruch/hackernews-client/tree/4.5

State Management in React and beyond

You have already learned the basics of state management in React in the previous chapters. This chapter digs a bit deeper into the topic. You will learn best practices, how to apply them and why you could consider using a third-party state management library.

Lifting State

Only the App component is a stateful ES6 component in your application. It handles a lot of application state and logic in its class methods. Maybe you have noticed that you pass a lot of properties to your Table component. Most of these props are only used in the Table component. In conclusion one could argue that it makes no sense that the App component knows about them.

The whole sort functionality is only used in the Table component. You could move it into the Table component, because the App component doesn't need to know about it at all. The process of refactoring substate from one component to another is known as *lifting state*. In your case, you want to move state that isn't used in the App component into the Table component. The state moves down from parent to child component.

In order to deal with state and class methods in the Table component, it has to become an ES6 class component. The refactoring from functional stateless component to ES6 class component is straight forward.

Your Table component as a functional stateless component:

src/App.js

```
const Table = ({
  list,
  sortKey,
  isSortReverse,
  onSort,
  onDismiss
}) => {
  const sortedList = SORTS[sortKey](list);
  const reverseSortedList = isSortReverse
    ? sortedList.reverse()
    : sortedList;

  return(
    ...
  );
}
```

Your Table component as an ES6 class component:

State Management in React and beyond

src/App.js

```
class Table extends Component {
  render() {
    const {
      list,
      sortKey,
      isSortReverse,
      onSort,
      onDismiss
    } = this.props;

    const sortedList = SORTS[sortKey](list);
    const reverseSortedList = isSortReverse
      ? sortedList.reverse()
      : sortedList;

    return(
      ...
    );
  }
}
```

Since you want to deal with state and methods in your component, you have to add a constructor and initial state.

src/App.js

```
class Table extends Component {
  constructor(props) {
    super(props);

    this.state = {};
  }

  render() {
    ...
  }
}
```

Now you can move state and class methods regarding the sort functionality from your App component down to your Table component.

src/App.js

```
class Table extends Component {
  constructor(props) {
    super(props);

    this.state = {
      sortKey: 'NONE',
      isSortReverse: false,
    };

    this.onSort = this.onSort.bind(this);
  }

  onSort(sortKey) {
    const isSortReverse = this.state.sortKey === sortKey && !this.state.isSortRe\
verse;
    this.setState({ sortKey, isSortReverse });
  }

  render() {
    ...
  }
}
```

Don't forget to remove the moved state and onSort() class method from your App component.

src/App.js

```
class App extends Component {
  constructor(props) {
    super(props);

    this.state = {
      results: null,
      searchKey: '',
      searchTerm: DEFAULT_QUERY,
      error: null,
      isLoading: false,
    };

    this.setSearchTopStories = this.setSearchTopStories.bind(this);
```

```
    this.fetchSearchTopStories = this.fetchSearchTopStories.bind(this);
    this.onDismiss = this.onDismiss.bind(this);
    this.onSearchSubmit = this.onSearchSubmit.bind(this);
    this.onSearchChange = this.onSearchChange.bind(this);
    this.needsToSearchTopStories = this.needsToSearchTopStories.bind(this);
  }

  ...

}
```

Additionally, you can make the Table component API more lightweight. Remove the props that are passed to it from the App component, because they are handled internally in the Table component now.

src/App.js

```
class App extends Component {

  ...

  render() {
    const {
      searchTerm,
      results,
      searchKey,
      error,
      isLoading
    } = this.state;

    ...

    return (
      <div className="page">
        ...
        <Table
          list={list}
          onDismiss={this.onDismiss}
        />
        ...
      </div>
    );
```

    }
}

Now in your Table component you can use the internal onSort() method and the internal Table state.

src/App.js

```
class Table extends Component {

  ...

  render() {
    const {
      list,
      onDismiss
    } = this.props;

    const {
      sortKey,
      isSortReverse,
    } = this.state;

    const sortedList = SORTS[sortKey](list);
    const reverseSortedList = isSortReverse
      ? sortedList.reverse()
      : sortedList;

    return(
      <div className="table">
        <div className="table-header">
          <span style={{ width: '40%' }}>
            <Sort
              sortKey={'TITLE'}
              onSort={this.onSort}
              activeSortKey={sortKey}
            >
              Title
            </Sort>
          </span>
          <span style={{ width: '30%' }}>
            <Sort
              sortKey={'AUTHOR'}
```

```
            onSort={this.onSort}
            activeSortKey={sortKey}
          >
            Author
          </Sort>
        </span>
        <span style={{ width: '10%' }}>
          <Sort
            sortKey={'COMMENTS'}
            onSort={this.onSort}
            activeSortKey={sortKey}
          >
            Comments
          </Sort>
        </span>
        <span style={{ width: '10%' }}>
          <Sort
            sortKey={'POINTS'}
            onSort={this.onSort}
            activeSortKey={sortKey}
          >
            Points
          </Sort>
        </span>
        <span style={{ width: '10%' }}>
          Archive
        </span>
      </div>
      { reverseSortedList.map((item) =>
        ...
      )}
    </div>
  );
  }
}
```

Your application should still work. But you made a crucial refactoring. You moved functionality and state closer into another component. Other components got more lightweight again. Additionally the component API of the Table got more lightweight because it deals internally with the sort functionality.

The process of lifting state can go the other way as well: from child to parent component. It is called as lifting state up. Imagine you were dealing with internal state in a child component. Now you want to fulfill a requirement to show the state in your parent component as well. You would have to lift up the state to your parent component. But it goes even further. Imagine you want to show the state in a sibling component of your child component. Again you would have to lift the state up to your parent component. The parent component deals with the internal state, but exposes it to both child components.

Exercises:

- read more about lifting state in React[124]
- read more about lifting state in learn React before using Redux[125]

---

[124] https://facebook.github.io/react/docs/lifting-state-up.html
[125] https://www.robinwieruch.de/learn-react-before-using-redux/

Revisited: setState()

So far, you have used React `setState()` to manage your internal component state. You can pass an object to the function where you can update partially the internal state.

Code Playground

```
this.setState({ foo: bar });
```

But `setState()` doesn't take only an object. In its second version, you can pass a function to update the state.

Code Playground

```
this.setState((prevState, props) => {
  ...
});
```

Why should you want to do that? There is one crucial use case where it makes sense to use a function over an object. It is when you update the state depending on the previous state or props. If you don't use a function, the internal state management can cause bugs.

But why does it cause bugs to use an object over a function when the update depends on the previous state or props? The React `setState()` method is asynchronous. React batches `setState()` calls and executes them eventually. It can happen that the previous state or props changed in between when you would rely on it in your `setState()` call.

Code Playground

```
const { fooCount } = this.state;
const { barCount } = this.props;
this.setState({ count: fooCount + barCount });
```

Imagine that `fooCount` and `barCount`, thus the state or the props, change somewhere else asynchronously when you call `setState()`. In a growing application, you have more than one 'setState()' call across your application. Since `setState()` executes asynchronously, you could rely in the example on stale values.

With the function approach, the function in `setState()` is a callback that operates on the state and props at the time of executing the callback function. Even though `setState()` is asynchronous, with a function it takes the state and props at the time when it is executed.

Code Playground

```
this.setState((prevState, props) => {
  const { fooCount } = prevState;
  const { barCount } = props;
  return { count: fooCount + barCount };
});
```

Now, lets get back to your code to fix this behavior. Together we will fix it for one place where setState() is used and relies on the state or props. Afterward, you are able to fix it at other places too.

The setSearchTopStories() method relies on the previous state and thus is a perfect example to use a function over an object in setState(). Right now, it looks like the following code snippet.

src/App.js

```
setSearchTopStories(result) {
  const { hits, page } = result;
  const { searchKey, results } = this.state;

  const oldHits = results && results[searchKey]
    ? results[searchKey].hits
    : [];

  const updatedHits = [
    ...oldHits,
    ...hits
  ];

  this.setState({
    results: {
      ...results,
      [searchKey]: { hits: updatedHits, page }
    },
    isLoading: false
  });
}
```

You extract values from the state, but update the state depending on the previous state asynchronously. Now you can use the functional approach to prevent bugs because of a stale state.

State Management in React and beyond 175

src/App.js

```
setSearchTopStories(result) {
  const { hits, page } = result;

  this.setState(prevState => {
    ...
  });
}
```

You can move the whole block that you have already implemented into the function. You only have to exchange that you operate on the prevState rather than this.state.

src/App.js

```
setSearchTopStories(result) {
  const { hits, page } = result;

  this.setState(prevState => {
    const { searchKey, results } = prevState;

    const oldHits = results && results[searchKey]
      ? results[searchKey].hits
      : [];

    const updatedHits = [
      ...oldHits,
      ...hits
    ];

    return {
      results: {
        ...results,
        [searchKey]: { hits: updatedHits, page }
      },
      isLoading: false
    };
  });
}
```

That will fix the issue with a stale state. There is one more improvement. Since it is a function, you can extract the function for an improved readability. That's one more advantage to use a function

State Management in React and beyond   176

over an object. The function can live outside of the component. But you have to use a higher order function to pass the result to it. After all, you want to update the state based on the fetched result from the API.

src/App.js

```
setSearchTopStories(result) {
  const { hits, page } = result;
  this.setState(updateSearchTopStoriesState(hits, page));
}
```

The `updateSearchTopStoriesState()` function has to return a function. It is a higher order function. You can define this higher order function outside of your App component. Note how the function signature changes slightly now.

src/App.js

```
const updateSearchTopStoriesState = (hits, page) => (prevState) => {
  const { searchKey, results } = prevState;

  const oldHits = results && results[searchKey]
    ? results[searchKey].hits
    : [];

  const updatedHits = [
    ...oldHits,
    ...hits
  ];

  return {
    results: {
      ...results,
      [searchKey]: { hits: updatedHits, page }
    },
    isLoading: false
  };
};

class App extends Component {
  ...
}
```

That's it. The function over an object approach in `setState()` fixes potential bugs yet increases readability and maintainability of your code. Furthermore, it becomes testable outside of the App component. You could export it and write a test for it as exercise.

Exercise:

- read more about React using state correctly[126]
- refactor all `setState()` methods to use a function
    - but only when it makes sense, because it relies on props or state
- run your tests again and verify that everything is up to date

---

[126] https://facebook.github.io/react/docs/state-and-lifecycle.html#using-state-correctly

Taming the State

The previous chapters have shown you that state management can be a crucial topic in larger applications. In general, not only React but a lot of SPA frameworks struggle with it. Applications got more complex in the recent years. One big challenge in web applications nowadays is to tame and control the state.

Compared to other solutions, React already made a big step forward. The unidirectional data flow and a simple API to manage state in a component are indispensable. These concepts make it easier to reason about your state and your state changes. It makes it easier to reason about it on a component level and to a certain degree on a application level.

In a growing application, it gets harder to reason about state changes. You can introduce bugs by operating on stale state when using an object over a function in `setState()`. You have to lift state around to share necessary or hide unnecessary state across components. It can happen that a component needs to lift up state, because its sibling component depends on it. Perhaps the component is far away in the component tree and thus you have to share the state across the whole component tree. In conclusion components get involved to a greater extent in state management. But after all, the main responsibility of components should be representing the UI, shouldn't it?

Because of all these reasons, there exist standalone solutions to take care of the state management. These solutions are not only used in React. However, that's what makes the React ecosystem such a powerful place. You can use different solutions to solve your problems. To address the problem of scaling state management, you might have heard of the libraries Redux[127] or MobX[128]. You can use either of these solutions in a React application. They come with extensions, react-redux[129] and mobx-react[130], to integrate them into the React view layer.

Redux and MobX are outside of the scope of this book. When you have finished the book, you will get guidance on how you can continue to learn React and its ecosystem. One learning path could be to learn Redux. Before you dive into the topic of external state management, I can recommend to read this article[131]. It aims to give you a better understanding of how to learn external state management.

Exercises:

- read more about external state management and how to learn it[132]
- check out my second ebook about state management in React[133]

---

[127] http://redux.js.org/docs/introduction/
[128] https://mobx.js.org/
[129] https://github.com/reactjs/react-redux
[130] https://github.com/mobxjs/mobx-react
[131] https://www.robinwieruch.de/redux-mobx-confusion/
[132] https://www.robinwieruch.de/redux-mobx-confusion/
[133] https://roadtoreact.com/

You have learned advanced state management in React! Let's recap the last chapters:

- React
    - lift state management up and down to suitable components
    - setState can use a function to prevent stale state bugs
    - existing external solutions that help you to tame the state

You can find the source code in the official repository[134].

[134] https://github.com/rwieruch/hackernews-client/tree/4.6

Final Steps to Production

The last chapters will show you how to deploy your application to production. You will use the free hosting service Heroku. On the way to deploy your application, you will learn more about *create-react-app*.

Eject

The following step and knowledge is **not necessary** to deploy your application to production. Still, I want to explain it to you. *create-react-app* comes with one feature to keep it extendable but also to prevent a vendor lock-in. A vendor lock-in usually happens when you buy into a technology but there is no escape hatch of using it in the future. Fortunately in *create-react-app* you have such an escape hatch with "eject".

In your *package.json* you will find the scripts to *start*, *test* and *build* your application. The last script is *eject*. You could try it, but there is no way back. **It is a one-way operation. Once you eject, you can't go back!** If you just started to learn React, it makes no sense to leave the convenient environment of *create-react-app*.

If you would run `npm run eject`, the command would copy all the configuration and dependencies to your *package.json* and a new *config/* folder. You would convert the whole project into a custom setup with tooling that includes Babel and Webpack. After all, you would have full control over all these tools.

The official documentation says that *create-react-app* is suitable for small to mid size projects. You shouldn't feel obligated to use the "eject" command.

Exercises:

- read more about eject[135]

---

[135] https://github.com/facebookincubator/create-react-app#converting-to-a-custom-setup

Deploy your App

In the end, no application should stay on localhost. You want to go live. Heroku is a platform as a service where you can host your application. They offer a seamless integration with React. To be more specific: It's possible to deploy a *create-react-app* in minutes. It is a zero-configuration deployment which follows the philosophy of *create-react-app*.

You need to fulfill two requirements before you can deploy your application to Heroku:

- install the Heroku CLI[136]
- create a free Heroku account[137]

If you have installed Homebrew, you can install the Heroku CLI from command line:

Command Line

```
brew update
brew install heroku-toolbelt
```

Now you can use git and Heroku CLI to deploy your application.

Command Line

```
git init
heroku create -b https://github.com/mars/create-react-app-buildpack.git
git add .
git commit -m "react-create-app on Heroku"
git push heroku master
heroku open
```

That's it. I hope your application is up and running now. If you run into problems you can check the following resources:

- Git and GitHub Essentials[138]
- Deploying React with Zero Configuration[139]
- Heroku Buildpack for create-react-app[140]

---

[136] https://devcenter.heroku.com/articles/heroku-command-line
[137] https://www.heroku.com/
[138] https://www.robinwieruch.de/git-essential-commands/
[139] https://blog.heroku.com/deploying-react-with-zero-configuration
[140] https://github.com/mars/create-react-app-buildpack

Outline

That was the last chapter of the book. I hope you enjoyed reading it and that it helped you to get traction in React. If you liked the book, share it as a way to learn React with your friends. It should be used as giveaway.

But where can you go from here after reading this book? You can either extend the application on your own or give your own React project a shot. Before you dive into another book, course or tutorial, you should create your own hands-on React project. Do it for one week, take it to production by deploying it somewhere, and reach out to me on Twitter[141] to showcase it. I am curious what you will build after you have read the book and I will gladly share it with my followers. You can also find me on GitHub[142] to share your repository.

If you are looking for further extensions for your application, I can recommend several learning paths after you have used only plain React in this book:

- **State Management**: You have used React `this.setState()` and `this.state` to manage and access local component state. That's a perfect start. However, in a larger application you will experience the limits of React's local component state[143]. Therefore you can use a third-party state management library such as Redux or MobX[144]. On the course platform Road to React[145], you will find the course "Taming the State in React" that teaches advanced local state in React, Redux and MobX. The course comes with an ebook as well, but I recommend everyone to dive into the source code and screencasts too. If you liked this book, you should definitely checkout Taming the State in React.
- **Sample Projects**: After learning plain React, it is always good to apply the learnings first in your own projects before learning something new. You could write your own tic-tac-toe game or a simple calculator in React. There are plenty of tutorials out there that use only React to build something exciting. Check out mine about building a paginated and infinite scrolling list[146], showcasing tweets on a Twitter wall[147] or connecting your React application to Stripe for charging money[148]. Experiment with these mini applications to get comfortable in React.
- **Code Organization**: On your way reading the book you came across one chapter about code organization. You could apply these changes now, if you haven't done it yet. It will organize your components in structured files and folders (modules). In addition, it helps to understand and learn the principles of code splitting, reusability, maintainability and module API design.

---

[141] https://twitter.com/rwieruch
[142] https://github.com/rwieruch
[143] https://www.robinwieruch.de/learn-react-before-using-redux/
[144] https://www.robinwieruch.de/redux-mobx-confusion/
[145] https://roadtoreact.com/
[146] https://www.robinwieruch.de/react-paginated-list/
[147] https://www.robinwieruch.de/react-svg-patterns/
[148] https://www.robinwieruch.de/react-express-stripe-payment/

- **Testing:** The book only scratched the surface of testing. If you are not familiar with the general topic, you could dive deeper into the concepts of unit testing and integration testing, especially in context of React applications. On an implementation level, I would recommend to stick to Enzyme and Jest in order to refine your approach of testing with unit tests and snapshot tests in React.
- **Asynchronous Requests:** You can substitute the native fetch API with third-party alternatives to perform asynchronous requests: superagent[149] or axios[150]. There is no perfect solution to make asynchronous requests. But by exchanging the buildings blocks around React, you make the experience how powerful it can be to have this flexibility[151]. In frameworks you usually stick to one solution. In a flexible ecosystem like React[152] you can exchange the solutions.
- **Routing:** You can implement routing for your application with react-router[153]. So far, you only have one page in your application. React Router helps you to have multiple pages across multiple URLs. When you introduce routing to your application, you don't make any requests to your web server to fetch the next page. The router will do everything for you on the client-side.
- **Type Checking:** In one chapter, you have used React PropTypes to define component interfaces. It is a good practice to prevent bugs. But the PropTypes are only checked on runtime. You can go one step further to introduce static type checking on compile time. TypeScript[154] is one popular approach. But in the React ecosystem, people often use Flow[155]. I can recommend to give Flow a shot if you are interested to make your application more robust.
- **Tooling with Webpack and Babel:** In the book you have used *create-react-app* to set up your application. At some point, when you have learned React, you might want to learn the tooling around it. It enables you to setup your own project without *create-react-app*. I can recommend to follow a minimal setup with Webpack and Babel[156]. Afterward you can apply more tooling on your own. For instance, you could use ESLint[157] to follow a unified code style in your application.
- **React Native:** React Native[158] brings your application on mobile devices. You can apply your learnings from React to ship iOS and Android applications. The learning curve, once you have learned React, shouldn't be steep in React Native. Both share the same principles. You will only encounter different layout components on mobile than you are used to in web applications.

---

[149] https://github.com/visionmedia/superagent
[150] https://github.com/mzabriskie/axios
[151] https://www.robinwieruch.de/reasons-why-i-moved-from-angular-to-react/
[152] https://www.robinwieruch.de/essential-react-libraries-framework/
[153] https://github.com/ReactTraining/react-router
[154] https://www.typescriptlang.org/
[155] https://flowtype.org/
[156] https://www.robinwieruch.de/minimal-react-webpack-babel-setup/
[157] https://www.robinwieruch.de/react-eslint-webpack-babel/
[158] https://facebook.github.io/react-native/

In general, I invite you to visit my website[159] to find more interesting topics about web development and software engineering. You can subscribe[160] to get updates roughly every month to your inbox and you can decide to support this kind of content by being my Patron[161]. Furthermore, the course platform Road to React[162] offers more advanced courses to learn about the React ecosystem. You should check it out!

Once again, if you liked the book, I want you to take a moment to think about a person who would be a good match to learn React. Reach out to that person and share the book. It would mean a lot to me. The book is intended to be given to others. It will improve over time when more people read it and share their feedback with me.

Thank you a lot for reading the Road to learn React.

Robin

---

[159] https://www.robinwieruch.de/
[160] https://www.getrevue.co/profile/rwieruch
[161] https://www.patreon.com/rwieruch
[162] https://roadtoreact.com/

Printed in Poland
by Amazon Fulfillment
Poland Sp. z o.o., Wrocław